T0194097

AGAINST ATHEISM

AGAINST ATHEISM

AND ITS SCIENTIFIC
AND RATIONAL PRETENSIONS

OSCAR PRIYANAND

WESTBOW
PRESS®
A DIVISION OF THOMAS NELSON
& ZONDERVAN

WestBow Press books may be ordered through booksellers or by contacting:

WestBow Press
A Division of Thomas Nelson & Zondervan
1663 Liberty Drive
Bloomington, IN 47403
www.westbowpress.com
1 (866) 928-1240

Scripture taken from the King James Version of the Bible.

ISBN: 978-1-9736-1870-6 (sc)
ISBN: 978-1-9736-1869-0 (hc)
ISBN: 978-1-9736-1871-3 (e)

Library of Congress Control Number: 2018901475

Print information available on the last page.

WestBow Press rev. date: 2/26/2019

AGAINST ATHEISM
AND ITS SCIENTIFIC
AND RATIONAL PRETENSIONS

CONTENTS

"Mene, Mene, Tekel, Upharsin."

Daniel 5:25

DEFINITIONS

I t is important to define the terms used in this book.

The Oxford advanced learners dictionary defines God as "…the being or spirit that is worshipped and is believed to have created the universe." Since most of the arguments of the atheists are against a Creator God, we will go by this definition in the book.

Theism, atheism, and *agnosticism* are easily defined by the answer one gives to the question "Does God exist?" There can be only three answers: yes, no, or don't know. A person who says "yes" is a theist, one who says "no" is an atheist, and one who says "I don't know" is an agnostic. Ironically, many militant atheists, including Michael Shermer and Richard Dawkins, admit they are actually agnostic when probed deeper. If they really are agnostic, then how come they are called "militant atheists" and are writing books like *God Is Not Great* and *The God Delusion*? We will have nothing to do with such chicanery in this book.

Pantheism is the belief that God is immanent in nature, and *deism* is the belief that although God created the universe, He does not intervene in its everyday workings. Both these worldviews deny the possibility of miracles. Even though both of these may differ from *theism*—a belief that God not only exists but also intervenes in its workings whenever required—they are all subdivisions under belief and not unbelief. In sharp contrast, atheism is an outright rejection of the existence of God and has nothing to do with either pantheism or deism. It is disingenuous of the atheists to call pantheists and deists as atheists who lack courage.

In the context of this debate, we will define "random" and "chance" to mean disorderly and unplanned. We must bear in mind that in the scientific context, nothing can be random in a universe that is governed by fixed laws of nature. Chance, luck, fluke, and random are mere English words devoid of any meaning in science except at the quantum level. Appealing to randomness and chance is not only antithetical to science but is against the very spirit of scientific enquiry. Any theory therefore appealing to random chance ceases to be scientific.

This book will avoid all scientific speculations which do not have empirical evidence to support them and focuses on the brute facts that we currently know. This is very important when it comes to interpreting the available evidence. Speculations are the creative imaginations of the theorists who conceive them and we will have nothing to do with those until we get sufficient empirical evidence.

We will use ethics and morals to mean the same thing even though there are subtle differences between them. A religion is defined not only by its belief in a creator God, but also by the moral code of conduct that it follows. If anyone professes a particular religion, then he is bound by the code of conduct of that religion. A Christian is therefore determined by the fruits of his action and not by what he outwardly professes to be. Christ himself taught a parable on how He will refuse to recognize those who profess His name but fail to live by His commandments. A Christian is therefore one who unwaveringly follows the teachings of Christ. If one were to deviate from those teachings, then one would, by definition, cease to be a Christian at that very instant. Viewed this way, even the Spanish Inquisition was as unchristian as can be. One cannot blame Christianity for everything that Christians do, especially when they do something that is contrary to the very moral code that they profess to follow. As it is written in 1 John 2:19, "They went out from us, but they were not of us."

This book defends the monotheistic God of the Holy Bible. Likewise, any mention of fairies, goblins, flying spaghetti monsters, Zeus, and Thor is equally ridiculed by us. In fact, Romans called Christians as atheists precisely because they did not believe in any of their mythical gods. It is therefore disingenuous of the atheists to bring up such primitive notions of God while debating Christian apologists. It is like ridiculing modern science by looking at its antecedents in astrology and alchemy. Utterly anachronistic to say the least.

There is also no point in bringing up examples of Islamic extremism when debating with Christian apologists. It is something which even Christianity condemns. Sometimes they conveniently cherry-pick and criticize verses from the Old Testament, which for Christians is a mere shadow of the deeper truths that were revealed by Christ in the New Testament. They can argue against Jihad and quote Old Testament when they are debating with Islamic or Jewish scholars, but not with Christians who believe in Jesus Christ and follow precepts laid down by Him alone.

INTRODUCTION

Trivialize and dismiss is the modus operandi of the militant atheists. This should be very obvious to anyone who cares to read their books or watch their debates. Their strident smart talk and rational pretensions have a following whose numbers are unfortunately increasing. Aided by vitriolic debates and books of the four horsemen of militant atheism—Richard Dawkins, Daniel Dennett, Sam Harris, and late Christopher Hitchens—they are becoming more vocal by the day.

Historically, atheism has always been lame and puerile—not that it is any more potent today—but what makes this new kid on the block different is its scientific and rational pretensions. To the extent that all their books and websites are more about science, its methodology, and its progress rather than about atheism itself. Science is one red herring that they use very effectively in their debates and books.

So far, the theistic response has been mainly from the Abrahamic religions with Christianity on the forefront. This itself is a remarkable testimony of Christianity, that it can be defended even in this age of science and reason. Prior to the rise of militant atheism, the Christian response to atheism has been from Christian apologists like Norman Geisler and C. S. Lewis. But these days many more have taken the onus of responding to militant atheism. Those on the forefront are William Lane Craig, Ravi Zacharias, Alvin Plantinga, Frank Turek, and Dinesh D'souza in the Americas and John Polkinghorne, John Lennox, Richard Swinburne, Alister McGrath, and Keith Ward in the United Kingdom. The defence of frontline apologists has been Christian in word and spirit. Unfortunately, our meekness and forbearance have been perceived as a weakness. It is time to put to rest any such misconceptions the atheists may be having.

The word "Apologetics" is a derivative of the Greek word *apologia*, which means a verbal defence. Christian Apologetics began in the first century of Christianity to defend its faith and rebut older mythical conceptions of God. Among the different religions today, Christianity is unique in its claim to have a cohesive worldview which at the same time is open to scrutiny and criticism—compared to Islam that allows no room for introspection or criticism whereas most polytheistic religions are too vague and incoherent to be defined and scrutinized.

We will take a radically different approach in Christian Apologetics. Instead of defending theism, we will go on a counter-offensive against atheism in this book, a *antepíthesi* (Greek for counter-offensive) of sorts. Instead of using traditional arguments to defend the existence of God—except for the Cosmological Argument which we will use briefly in the beginning—we will go on the offensive and show how unscientific and irrational the atheistic worldview is. In the end, even if this book does not convince you to be a Bible-thumping believer, it will make it impossible for you to be an atheist.

This book will argue that science and rationality have its origins in a Christian theistic worldview and that the evidence from science for a Creator God is simply overwhelming. We will also make a strong case that both atheism and science have nothing to do with morality. In the absence of a moral compass, science needs religion—specifically Christianity—more than ever to give it a direction. We will also briefly show why Christianity is unique among all the religions of the world and make a strong case that it alone can provide the rational foundation for peaceful and tolerant nations.

If there was a single event that pushed me to write this book, then it was the Oxford Union debate on November 8, 2014 to defend the proposition: "This house believes in God." But unfortunately, they did not have the right people defending this proposition except for John Lennox, professor of Mathematics and Philosophy at the University of Oxford, while the atheistic side had their best representatives in Dan Barker, Michael Shermer, and Peter Millican. I wonder why the best in theistic defence like Norman Geisler, Frank Turek, William Lane Craig, and Ravi Zacharias were not invited to the debate. Needless to say, the proposition failed to pass even when the atheistic defence was mediocre at its best. Although this whole book is a rebuttal of what they have said during that debate, the last chapter (If I were in Oxford on that day) contains what I would have said if I were around on that day. If you are hard pressed for time, this chapter along with the summaries at the end of each chapter will give you a good overview of the entire book.

Finally, we will end the book with an FAsQ (Frequently Asked stupid Questions) section, where we will answer some of the most common questions which every atheist repeats like a parrot.

This book is written with extreme urgency and as such its tone may be straight forward to the point of being rude. Suffice it to say that the arguments will be presented without any sugarcoating. But if anyone thinks we are being overly blunt, then they should flip through a few pages of books written by the militant atheists to see the scorn and contempt they have for God and religion. It is high time we returned those compliments. I strongly believe that in our quest for truth, we should keep all etiquette aside.

This book is also intended to be short and concise for the sake of today's generation. Our concern for them is paramount. They are the ones who are most vulnerable to the scientific and rational pretensions of the militant atheists. We hope this book will enable them to understand that theism has a much stronger scientific and rational basis than atheism.

I have tried my best to keep out technical jargon (except in the chapter on evolution) so that anyone with fleeting interest can also understand the central message of this book. Most of the chapters are written so that they can be read and understood independently without referring to the other chapters, except when we discuss the incoherence among the atheists in the eighteenth chapter. Since each chapter is independent of others, there may be repetitive elements in them. The reader is advised to overlook those and focus on the central message that each chapter is conveying.

This book is specifically against the militant atheists and their arguments. Anyone not familiar with the typical smart talk of the four cowboys of militant atheism might not quite get the drift. I will try my best to set the context before giving the rebuttal but it would help if one were aware of their arguments beforehand.

Before we begin, it is important to set one record straight at the outset. Atheism is not a debate about methodologies or ethical frameworks. The common strategy of atheists is to sidetrack this debate into a discussion on scientific methodology or secular ethics. We will need to tread carefully here and avoid all such red herrings that distract us. Even though we will answer the questions of methodology and ethics later in the book, we should remember that atheism by definition is a specific claim that God does not exist. It is that specific claim that we will utterly demolish both scientifically and rationally in this book.

In the Beginning

I think, therefore I exist.

I exist, but I did not create myself.

Therefore, there exists an entity that created me.

You could point to my parents and claim they have created me, or you could point to a complex process like morphogenesis and attribute my existence to it. Although there is an element of truth in both these deductions and is useful to see the causal relationships, we think that they are ultimately petty, trivial, and myopic when one is trying to answer the deeper questions of existence. By pointing to the immediate preceding cause, we are merely passing the buck, because one could then go on to ask who created my parents or how the process of morphogenesis came to be in the first place?

Unfortunately, all scientific explanations are of this passing the buck type. Peter Atkins, former professor of chemistry at the University of Oxford, an obdurate atheist, is the master of such "nothing but" trivializations. One just needs to flip through a few pages of his book *Creation revisited: The Origin of Space, Time and the Universe* to see a sample of such petty explanations.

The deeper question is whether such superficial explanations are enough to explain the origins of our universe and life? We don't think so. Consider the following thought experiment. Suppose I set up a detailed contraption that at the touch of a button from another country sets off the trigger of a remote-controlled gun to shoot and kill a certain deluded retired zoologist in Oxford. If Peter Atkins were the judge, he would say "nothing but" the bullet had killed the zoologist and close the case. But investigators with a little more common sense will not buy such myopic deductions. Instead, they will do a detailed investigation and trace the contraption to me—the first cause—and bring me to justice.

In the same way, the first cause is the root cause of our existence. We owe our very existence to it. No matter how atheists like Atkins try to dismiss the first cause using a "nothing but" trivialization, the undeniable fact is that it had the wisdom and potential to create a universe that can go on to make you and me.

The fundamental question we should then be asking is how did the first cause come to be in the first place? Science cannot bail us out here because of its causal method. Every effect must have a cause. Such a trail of causal explanations invariably ends up in a *reductio ad absurdum ad infinitum*. It is turtles all the way down for them.

The first cause therefore can have only two logical answers and both of them are preternatural. When all the possibilities are eliminated, only the impossible remain. Either an entity created itself and then created us or we are the product of an eternally existing entity. Whatever that entity is or whatever science chooses to label such an entity, we revere that entity as our Creator God. Was there some first principle that created us? Then for us that is "In the beginning was the Word…and the Word was God…All things were made by him…" (Gospel of Saint John 1:1-3.) This rational deduction is inevitable.

Whatever it takes to create our incredible universe, the first cause had to have those in place. Science currently tells us that it takes incredible power, universal order, and great wisdom to create a universe that is stable enough to create us. This trinity is essential for our existence.

Albert Einstein showed us that matter and energy are interconvertible. The atom bomb converts very small amount of matter to incredible amount of energy. Conversely, it takes immense amount of energy to create just a spoonful of sugar. Imagine then, the colossal amount of energy that would be needed to create our vast universe that is currently estimated to have two trillion galaxies each of which contains about one- to four-hundred billion stars.

Secondly, we also see a universal order in the universe. These immutable laws and constants of physics have become the axioms and postulates of science. We know that these laws of physics are omnipresent and omnipotent in the universe. They make our universe the way it is and guide matter and energy to make stars, planets, you, and me. And forces that guide the universe in a specific direction is exactly what one should expect to observe in a teleological universe. Without these laws, our universe would not only be chaotic but would also be incomprehensible to the scientists.

Thirdly, it takes great wisdom to fine-tune those laws and constants of physics to create a stable universe like ours that can go on to support life. Even the tiniest of variations would have made it impossible for our universe to support life. Perhaps an example would help. If the Gravitational constant would vary in one part in 10^{60} (that is one part in 1 followed by 60 zeroes) then life would not have existed. When this dawned on the physicist Fred Hoyle, the English astronomer remarked, "A common sense interpretation of the facts suggest that a super-intellect has monkeyed with physics as well as with chemistry and biology and that there are no blind forces worth speaking about in nature. The number one calculates from the facts seem to me so overwhelming as to put this conclusion (of fine-tuning) almost beyond question."

Sir Martin Rees, astronomer royal of Great Britain and emeritus professor of cosmology and astrophysics at the University of Cambridge notes that wherever physicists look, they see examples of fine-tuning. David Deutch, a physicist at the University of Oxford says, "If anyone claims not to be surprised by the special features that the universe has, he is hiding his head in the sand. These special features are surprising and unlikely."

The first cause then should have incredible power, an ability to bring about order, and wisdom to bring about a universe that can create us. Ironically, these are the very attributes we ascribe unto God. We have not only deduced what it takes to create this universe, but have also connected the dots about the nature of the first cause—infinitely powerful, capable, and wise. As mentioned before, whatever science chooses to call the first cause or the eternal source of creation (if the universe turns out to be eternal), we revere that entity as our Creator God. The only difference between science and religion then is in the nomenclature.

But it is amusing to see the fumbling answers which atheists give to explain this incredible power, order, and wisdom that we find in the universe. Lawrence Krauss, the American theoretical physicist and cosmologist thinks it is "plausible" that our universe could have popped out of absolutely nothing. They also postulate that the laws of physics which bring about the order found in nature are somehow "inherent." And to explain the wisdom found in fine-tuning, they resort to speculative myths like the multiverse or parallel universes—which are highly speculative theories that currently have no empirical evidence whatsoever. In the next few paras we will examine how rational and scientific these atheistic excuses are.

Lawrence Krauss in his book *A Universe from Nothing: Why There is Something Rather than Nothing* uses the quantum "weirdness" to envisage a universe out of nothing. But the ground reality is that quantum physics is not science but the end thereof. Niels Bohr, one of the founders of quantum physics once remarked that those who are not shocked by the quantum theory, may not have actually understood it. Instead of calling it quantum physics, we should be calling it quantum magic.

It is flapdoodle to say that it is natural for something to pop out of nothing. If I were to put the entire universe on the right side of the equation and nothing on the left then that is definitely not natural science. It is pure magic. And it is exactly what one should expect in the Christian worldview and not in the materialistic worldview of an atheist. "...even God...*calleth* those things which be not as though they were." (Romans 4:17.)

The second reason that one cannot use quantum physics to explain the origin of the universe is because it is a logical contradiction. One cannot claim that the child begat the father rather than the other way around. Quantum phenomena and conditions are found in the universe post creation and could not have existed before creation. It is logically inconsistent to say that the child begat the father. Unless of course, they are telling us that the quantum condition transcends space and time. If it does then even that is miraculous. Why not we rename it as the God condition?

Thirdly, if the universe indeed can come out of nothing, could they kindly demonstrate it please? After all it takes nothing to create one, right? If they claim that we cannot detect it even if they are popping out of nothing then how does one know whether they are indeed popping into existence? Except by blind faith? Is this not the atheistic version of a fire-breathing dragon in the garage which Carl Sagan used to ridicule religion?

Fourthly, if they are proposing to use quantum physics to envisage a universe out of nothing, how do they plan to resolve the measurement problem that plagues quantum physics? As pointed out earlier, quantum physics is utterly weird. It is a brute fact of quantum phenomena that it takes an observer or a measurement to collapse the wave function. Instead of supporting atheism, the quantum condition is actually giving us incontrovertible proof of a Creator God—the observer. It is ironic that the atheists resort to a less parsimonious speculation of parallel universes to escape this inevitable conclusion.

It is important to note that the physicists themselves, including Nobel prize winners, disagree with Lawrence Krauss that the universe can be conjured out of absolutely nothing. This was evident in the discussion following his talk at the Nobel Conference 49 in Gustavus Adolphus College where no one but Krauss was belligerent in claiming that the universe could come out of absolutely nothing. A casual observer (you can watch it on YouTube) cannot help but be baffled at his smart talk during the conference. He may have a great sense of humour but pathetically fails to convince. James Gates, a string theorist from the University of Maryland questioned Krauss on the dynamics in the absence of time, and Frank Wilczek, a Nobel Laureate in physics, was clearly annoyed with the definition of "nothing" and insisted that they can only speculate within a framework, which of course is not nothing. Krauss had no answer for either of them except comedy and smart talk.

Lastly, how can we verify that our universe had indeed popped out of nothing? For aliens who have no clue about electromagnetic radiation, even the radio would seem to be blabbering out of nothing, and the television would seem to be hallucinating strange visions out of thin air.

We should also note that his book is not a peer-reviewed scientific paper but rather a highly speculative and deluded atheistic attempt to explain the origin of our universe. It has no support or consensus within the scientific community. Luke Barnes, a post-doctoral researcher in the University of Sydney in his blog *Letters to nature* had the following to say about Lawrence Krauss: "The book descends into the ridiculous. Krauss tells us that, "something" may not be very special or even very common in the multiverse. So, in the totality of physical existence, it might be that only some things are "something" but most things aren't. That is exactly as daft as it sounds. This nonsense has no warrant from modern cosmology."

While every sensible scientist is questioning this ridiculous notion of a universe out of nothing, he has a supporter in Richard Dawkins who also wrote the Afterword to Krauss' book. Michael Brooks while reviewing the book for New Scientist (a UK-based science magazine) rightly observed that the Afterword was downright superfluous and silly. It is appalling to see a person like Dawkins who was elected to be the Simonyi professor for the public understanding of science, support such absurd views as a universe popping into existence out of absolutely nothing. Whichever committee that elected Richard Dawkins to chair that position needs to apologize to the general public for their irresponsible nomination. This man has created the greatest misunderstanding between science and religion in the history of modern science since Pierre-Simon Laplace. Francis Bacon, the father of the scientific method, rightly pointed out that a little science (read that as half knowledge) makes one an atheist but a deeper understanding of nature makes one turn to God. How remarkably true are those words for this generation.

Peter Atkins is even more ridiculous when it comes to conjuring up a universe out of nothing. In his book *Creation Revisited*, he lets his imagination run wild: "Now, at the time before time…Spacetime emerged by chance out of its own dust." He continues his flight of fancy…"Elsewhere (but there is no where yet) and at other times (but there is no time anywhere) the dust of spacetime happens to form itself into tiny universes of one dimension." It is clear from the above examples that when it comes to the crucial question of creation, the atheists blithely abandon their science and rationality. Such fanciful tales are no different from the creation myths and folklore found in ancient civilizations.

This atheistic delusion that the universe can pop out of absolutely nothing is clearly unscientific nonsense. It is neither observable nor demonstrable. It cannot be tested and verified nor can it make any predictions. Even if a test is proposed, nothing can be said or decided until the results are known. Current science will simply have nothing to do with such wild speculative myths. "Professing themselves to be wise, they became fools…" (Romans 1:22.)

Secondly, where are the atheists planning to get the universal order that governs the universe from? Every elementary particle like the neutron,

15

proton, and electron has the same properties no matter where they are formed in the universe. Their assumption that the laws of nature are inherent cannot be scientific either. How are the precise values of electrons and quarks derived? If the atheists want to claim that they are not derivative then those are magical as well. It is as though the electron will say "I am that I am" if we listen carefully!

More importantly, forces that guide the development of our universe is exactly what one would expect to see in a teleological universe. The fact that these forces have been fine tuned to create us, is further evidence that the universe was expecting us. As Fred Hoyle observed, there are no "blind forces" to speak of in nature. On the contrary, these forces are clockwork mechanisms that bring about the incredible beauty that we see in nature.

Thirdly, there is no cohesive or rational answer to the brute fact of fine-tuning in the atheistic camp. They either become Holocaust deniers or resort to speculations like infinite or parallel universes. Even if they choose to interpret the brute fact of fine-tuning differently, then at no point can they discount intelligent causation also as a valid interpretation. They are just being whimsical in not adopting the theistic interpretation.

Consider project SETI (Search for Extra-Terrestrial Intelligence.) If a puerile radio signal from outer space can be deemed as evidence of extra-terrestrial intelligence, then why can't the incredibly powerful evidence of fine-tuning be evidence for intelligent causation? Why the double standards?

Richard Dawkins thinks that we cannot postulate a complex intelligent entity like God to explain fine-tuning because it will be even more difficult to explain how such a powerful intelligence came to be in the first place. This is an utterly fallacious argument. If an alien lands on Mars and looks at the various robotic rovers we have sent to the planet, then the alien would rightly conclude intelligent causation even if it is unaware of how humans—who created them and who are much more complicated than the robotic rovers—came to be in the first place. Just because one cannot explain where the intelligence could have come from is no reason for discounting the intelligent causation itself. This is a *non sequitur* we have to do away with. And just because it is a headache for the atheists to envisage a complex entity like God, it is no excuse for denying the brute fact that it takes intelligence to do the fine-tuning.

Even the Big Bang was anything but simple. It was incredibly more ordered at the beginning than it is now. The beginning could even involve infinities which from the physics point of view are unresolvable problems. This is a brute fact of nature. It follows that the past was infinitely more ordered thermodynamically than the present and not the other way around. If Dawkins finds it hard to envisage this, then who cares? That is his personal incredulity.

Many scientists who are not involved in the God debate like Martin Rees and Leonard Susskind have confessed that one of the interpretations could be the existence of God. In fact, many atheists like Michael Shermer have admitted that fine-tuning is the best evidence that theism has for the existence of God. But for some whimsical reason which is neither scientific nor rational, they shy away from accepting it as conclusive evidence. Perhaps it is "nothing but" their whim that is preventing them from accepting this evidence for God.

Whimsical is the right word when one looks at the pandemonium of interpretations in the atheistic camp regarding the fine-tuning of our universe. Victor Stenger denied it altogether, Neil deGrasse Tyson reviles any such notion of fine-tuning, Richard Dawkins resorts to unproven speculations, and Sean Carroll has blind faith that it will be explained away in the future. The most bizarre reactions of all come from Anthony Grayling, Dan Barker, Arif Ahmed, and Douglas Adams—two of whom are armchair philosophers and not scientists. It is a waste of time to add even a paragraph to rebut their naive responses. When referring to scientific facts, one should consult scientists (we have already quoted what scientists like Martin Rees have said regarding fine-tuning) and not philosophers or comedians.

Atheists like Peter Atkins always strive to minimize the role of God in the universe. Not sure what they intend to achieve by doing that. Suppose there is a car engineer who designs an assembly line of sorts, who creates the raw materials out of nothing, who takes your colour options and other preferences into account and presses a few buttons to roll out a car of your choice without any human intervention. The world will call him an incredible genius and give him a Nobel Prize. But when God does it, they call Him lazy!

Many scientists who have a broader perspective of our universe believe in God. But most of them believe in a deistic God and shy away from believing in a theistic God. Deism could be as far as science can get and therefore be a limitation of science rather than of God. Einstein had the habit of saying "God does not play dice" whenever confronted with the quantum conundrum. In one of the conferences, Niels Bohr, one of the earliest proponents of quantum physics is supposed to have told Einstein not to tell God what to do. I think we could rephrase this for the atheists and deists as well: Don't tell God what *not* to do. That is, not to intervene in the workings of the universe.

Even if science is unwilling to go beyond the empirical universe and admit the existence of a transcendent God, it must ascribe all the attributes of God to the universe and nature itself: that it created itself or existed eternally; that power, order, and wisdom are immanent in nature; that the laws of physics which bring about order in the universe are both omnipresent and omnipotent; and that they are omniscient enough to be fine-tuned and bring us into existence. Ironically, it is the very view that pantheism holds. Since the only source of wisdom that we know is a conscious intelligence, this pantheism should transition into panpsychism—a view that consciousness, mind, or soul is a universal and primordial feature of all things. Scientific materialists have therefore unwittingly become high priests of panpsychism. Science then becomes the newest handmaiden of religion.

It should be clear to us by now that there is no place for atheism in the universe. We exist, but we did not create ourselves, therefore there exists an entity that created us. This creative agent is a self-evident truth. An axiom and postulate of our very existence. This creative agent must have the incredible power, order, and wisdom to not only create itself, but also to create the universe and us. Whatever science calls this creative agent, we revere that entity as our Creator God. The beginning of the universe therefore is the end of science and naturalism. "I am Alpha and Omega, the beginning and the end, the first and the last." (Rev 22:13.)

The debate therefore can only be on the nature of that Creator God— whether He is deistic, pantheistic, or theistic—and not on His existence. Atheists are welcome to assume that the universe came out of nothing, that the laws of physics are somehow inherent to nature, and the fine-tuning is sheer dumb luck, but they have no right to call such assumptions scientific or rational. If atheists want to abandon causality and claim that the universe can indeed come out of nothing and no cause then they are committing intellectual *hara-kiri*. In which case, we will have to order coffins for both science and naturalism. Atheists who rely on science and naturalism are welcome to join the requiem.

There are two ways in which deism can transition to theism—the origin of life and our free will. The origin of prokaryotes and eukaryotes—the atoms with which all life on earth is made of—has clear evidence of intelligent causation. These are William Paley's newest watches whose complexity implies a Watchmaker. The universe may be fine-tuned for sustaining life but it may not be enough to create life in the first place. An example might help: the functioning of an automobile engine can be reduced to physics and chemistry while its assembly cannot. Ditto in the case of life. We now know that life is not just physics and chemistry but also an information processing system. And all information systems are top-down design and not bottom-up. The assumption that life had randomly assembled itself cannot be a scientific one in any sense. Instead, these are atheistic assertions that we should do away with. Science is trying to comprehend order and processes found in nature and not resign to random chaos. It is therefore more rational to believe in the inevitability of intelligent causation than in the improbability of random chance.

A typical living cell in each of us is infinitely more complicated than any nanotechnology we have created so far. This is clear evidence of intelligent causation. Abiogenesis, the official scientific position on the origin of life has been repeatedly falsified in nature and in the laboratory ever since it was postulated more than a century ago. Even if scientists managed to create artificial life in the lab (which would probably be using the top-down approach), it is simply a *quod erat demonstrandum* (QED) for intelligent causation—in this case, for human intelligence.

Our free will is another miracle that we experience in our daily life. This makes our scientific enquiry "objective" and at the same time makes us morally responsible individuals. No physical system that is "nothing but" physics and chemistry can ever have free will. The present state of any physical system is the result of its previous state and the future is determined by its present. Yet we exercise free will every day of our lives and we have no clue how that can happen. If we leave aside the experimental difficulties in verifying whether we have free will or not, we must remember that scientific materialism cannot admit free will even in principle. And if they insist that we cannot have free will, then this debate is futile. They are shooting themselves in the foot by denying it. There cannot be any meaningful dialogue in the absence of free will. Unfortunately, even deism and pantheism cannot accommodate free will, which makes theism the most rationally consistent worldview of all.

Theism therefore is clearly a scientific and rational deduction. The greatest misunderstanding of this generation is that science validates atheism while the evidence is pointing to exactly the opposite direction. Atheism is simply not a viable option in context of the first cause. Denying God is denying the first cause which in turn is denying the scientific method of causality itself. Faith now seems redundant for this generation when we can rationally deduce the existence of God. Past generations who did not have the advancement of science may have needed faith to believe in God, but the current generation has no excuse because it has plenty of evidence pointing to a Creator who is powerful and intelligent. In the past, they needed miracles to be convinced, but for the present generation His ordinary works are more than sufficient. Whether one likes it or not, we are a product of an entity that miraculously created itself or had existed eternally.

Of all the three worldviews—theism, atheism, and agnosticism—it should be very clear to us that atheism and agnosticism are not even valid options. Denying the existence of our Creator is denying existence itself. Atheism is therefore the most unscientific and irrational position of all. And among all the three worldviews of belief—theism, deism, and pantheism—theism is clearly the most rationally consistent worldview of all. The only debate can now be on the nature of our Creator and not His existence.

In the Christian worldview, God is a Spirit (John 4:24.) Science currently has no way of detecting conscious entities, how then does it plan to detect God? Neither can science figure out the contents of a conscious mind. It cannot even predict the trajectory of a fly, how then does it plan to comprehend the mind of God? The only way we can know what is in the mind of a conscious entity is by revelation. No one can know, even if they poke electrodes into my skull—whether I prefer strawberry over vanilla—unless I choose to reveal it to them. Ditto for God. We can never know the contents of His mind unless He chooses to reveal it to us. And since God is not a "thing" but a person, it is His prerogative to reveal Himself to whomsoever He wills—His saints and prophets. We ignore them at our peril.

We sincerely hope the atheists are not thrusting electrodes into the heads of their spouses to get empirical evidence of their love. This is no way to develop a relationship. Ditto with God. If we want to develop a relationship with Him then we need to have faith and trust on Him. The whole world runs on faith and trust. While it takes methods of science—experiment and observation—to build cars and planes, it takes religious methods—faith and trust—to build relationships.

Every rational endeavour of comprehension takes for granted certain unprovable or irreducible axioms and postulates as self-evident. Mathematics has its own set of axioms and postulates which are used to generate theorems. Science takes for granted matter and the laws that govern it as its axioms and postulates to generate theories. Why then should the atheists object if theists take God as their axiom and postulate to generate a cohesive theology? Even if we are unable to explain how He came to be in the first place.

Not everyone might go to the extent of being religious theists, even if it is demonstrably the most rational choice of all. They may instead choose to stop at being pantheists or deists. All three are logical deductions. But can atheism profess any logical deductions like these? None so far as we can see. The rest of the book is *tour de force* to show why it is impossible to rationally justify atheism.

In Summary

We exist, but we did not create ourselves. Therefore, there exists an entity that created us. Science can point out to the immediate precedent causes but that may not be enough if we need to know the ultimate nature of existence. Since all scientific explanations pass the buck, they all lead to the mother of all causes—the first cause. Science can never help in resolving the problem of origins because of its causal methodology, it lapses into a *reduction ad absurdum*. The first cause then can have only two solutions and both of them are preternatural. Either some entity created itself and then created us or some eternally existing entity created us. The first cause or the eternal source is the root cause of my existence and whatever science chooses to call that entity, we revere that entity as our Creator God.

We know from science that it takes incredible power, order, and wisdom to create a universe like ours that can go on to make us. Even if science does not want to go beyond what they can empirically detect, they must ascribe all the attributes of God to the universe itself. That it is self-creating or eternally existing, powerful, capable, and wise enough to bring us into existence. In which case, science becomes natural theology.

The origin of life and free will makes a theistic worldview the only way out. The very fact that intelligent scientists are trying to create life in the lab is QED for intelligent causation and denying free will would render all debates useless and our science subjective and parochial.

According to the Bible, God is a spirit. The only way we can know what is in the mind of a conscious entity is by revelation since science has no way of knowing what a conscious person is thinking. According to the monotheistic worldview, God is a person, it is therefore His prerogative to reveal himself to whomsoever He wills—His saints and prophets—we ignore them at our peril.

Of all the worldviews on the existence of God—theism, atheism, and agnosticism—it is very clear that atheism is the least scientific and rational of all. And among the main systems of belief—deism, pantheism, and theism—it is clear that theism is the most scientific and rationally consistent of all.

WHAT DOES IT TAKE TO BE AN ATHEIST?

Nikita Khruschev, former first secretary of the Communist Party of the Soviet Union is rumored to have said during a plenum of the state's anti-religious campaign that "Gagarin flew into space, but didn't see any god there." We are just curious to know what kind of evidence did they expect to see of God from their capsule? Atlas carrying the globe on his shoulder? Or Rahu and Ketu swallowing the sun to cause eclipses? Or the earth supported on endless tortoises? All of which are primitive pre-Christian worldviews which we have done away with two millennia ago. In fact, in the first few centuries of the Christian era, Christians were called atheists precisely for not believing in these primitive Greek and Roman conceptions of God. The hubris of Khruschev's statement becomes even more evident when we step back and see the immensity of the cosmos that current telescopes have revealed to us and how little we have explored of it so far.

Even before we begin to explore the question of God's existence, we should first ask if we are capable of answering that question in the first place. Ironically, we simply cannot answer this question confidently in an atheistic worldview. According to their worldview, we are nothing but genetically modified apes, lumbering robots possessing half knowledge, and having no free will. How then does one expect such entities to answer these profound questions? Does anyone go to the zoo and ask such profound questions to the inmates therein? Or ask a calculator that has no free will and is made for something else like crunching numbers, whether it can detect its creator and expect a rational analysis of the same? Atheism is clearly self-defeating right at the outset. If atheism is right then atheism is wrong.

This paradox is so profound that we could just tell the atheists to speak no more and go home. But for now, we will keep aside this fundamental contradiction and believe that they are capable of free rational thought. What then in purely scientific and rational terms does it take to be an atheist? Plenty, as we shall see. The only scientific reason they give is the supposed "lack of evidence." Atheists like Dawkins and Grayling claim there is insufficient scientific evidence for the existence of God. But that could stem from our incomplete knowledge of the cosmos. If half knowledge is dangerous then it cannot be more dangerous than here. To promote a worldview with half knowledge is both unscientific and irrational to say the least. Instead, they should be saying "We don't know," which is quite different from saying "There is no evidence." If they really meant to confess that they don't know—which is an agnostic view—then how come they are called "militant atheists" and are writing books like *God Is Not Great* and *The God Delusion*? Either they are deluding themselves, or are not honest in their approach and are confusing the media and everyone who is interested in this debate.

Consider the example of SETI (Search for Extra-Terrestrial Intelligence) once again. Can anyone claim that there are no aliens in the universe? Many SETI enthusiasts tell us that it is arrogant to say that aliens don't exist even when they don't have a shred of evidence of their existence. If it is arrogant to say that aliens don't exist then why isn't it arrogant to say that God does not exist even after discovering solid evidence of power, order, and wisdom in the universe?

As mentioned earlier, scientists have been astonished at how finely tuned the laws of physics are for the universe to be stable enough to sustain life on earth. Even a miniscule change in those laws would have been devastating for life. This has given the believers enough rationale to believe in intelligent causation. Theism then stands clearly justified.

But is unbelief justifiable? It is important to note that we can justify our belief in the existence of something (Extra-Terrestrial Intelligence or God) with limited knowledge but cannot justify our unbelief while having half knowledge. Here is why. Suppose we receive a radio signal which is transmitting Newtonian equations, we can immediately conclude that ETI exists without searching further. For believers of ETI, the quest ends because they have limited but confirmed knowledge of their existence. They will cease from questioning if they exist or not and instead begin to speculate and debate on the nature of those aliens.

On the contrary, a disbeliever can never justify his unbelief until he has analyzed all the radio signals in the cosmos and found no intelligent signal among them. And for him to do that in space and time—deciphering all signals in the past, present, and future—he needs to be omnipresent in space and time, omniscient to be aware of all the radio signals, and omnipotent to parse the humongous amount of big data that will pour in. We know that these are the very qualities we attribute to God. In other words, it takes a God to say that there is no God! But we are puny mortals inhabiting a tiny speck of a planet in a remote corner of this infinite cosmos. Humanity will do well in steering clear from the hubris of these militant atheists.

If atheists are looking for material evidence of God, they need to search the material extent of the universe to conclude that He does not exist. Until they do that, they have the right to remain silent. Up against this wall of half knowledge, the atheists usually resort to pub talk like "celestial teapots." But is that a scientific methodology or a rational way of resolving the most important question for humanity? Absolutely not. These are puerile philosophical meanderings, the last resort of impatient ignoramuses.

Ironically, they are the ones who are believing in the existence of celestial teapots, the only difference is that they call them "flying saucers." They even believe in flying spaghetti monsters, but call them with slightly different names like Jabba the Hutt, Derkolo, Ewok, Chewbacca, Spock, and little green men. Search for ETI is based on the blind faith that there must be aliens out there even when they don't have a shred of empirical evidence for it. NASA has even wasted millions of dollars in sending probes and rovers to Mars with exactly this wild speculation based on nothing but blind faith.

In science, it is extremely annoying to see atheists conclude that there is no need of God even when their understanding of the cosmos and life, especially their origins is incomplete. We still do not understand how our cosmos and life began. In fact, we do not even understand the very entity we use to understand the universe—our conscious mind. Any conclusion therefore with incomplete knowledge cannot be justified and is against the very spirit of scientific enquiry. If they are not convinced by the current evidence presented by the theists, how do they know that science will never discover new overwhelming evidence for God? Who knows? A day may come when science will become indistinguishable with religion as it probes deeper into nature and consciousness.

Another stumbling block for atheists who use science to justify their unbelief is causality. One of the foundations of the scientific method is also its Achilles heel. Every effect must have a cause. This infinite regress of cause and effect will take forever to unravel and since there is always a possibility of discovering God in the process, they will have to wait forever to be an atheist. "Ever learning, and never able to come to the knowledge of the truth." (II Timothy 3:7.)

Thomas Kuhn, in his book *The Structure of Scientific Revolutions* gives one criterion of a valid scientific hypothesis: falsification. We propose that even our God hypothesis can be falsified if it can be shown that we created ourselves. In the absence of which, the only way to deny the existence of our Creator is to deny our own existence. "Because that, when they knew God, they glorified him not as God, neither were thankful, but became vain in their imaginations, and their foolish heart was darkened." (Romans 1:21.)

Key Summary

If we begin with an atheistic worldview, it is impossible for one to rationally answer the question of God's existence. Most atheists call us genetically modified apes who are optimized for survival and not rational thought. In their materialistic worldview, there cannot be any room for free will. In such a scenario, we cannot trust any of our rational deductions, including whether God exists or not. If atheism is right then atheism is wrong.

If atheists are looking for material evidence of God then they should survey the material extent of the universe to decide if God exists or not. More importantly, one can believe with half knowledge but cannot disbelieve while having half knowledge. Consider the example of project SETI (Search for Extra-Terrestrial Intelligence), one signal from outer space could prove the existence of aliens and we need not look any further. We have limited but confirmed knowledge of their existence. We can then go on to debate on the nature of those aliens rather on their existence.

But we cannot disbelieve the existence of aliens until we have searched the entire universe. This can happen only when one is omnipresent throughout the universe, omniscient of all the signals in the universe, and omnipotent to process all the signals past, present, and future to confirm the non-existence of aliens. Ditto in the case of God's existence. If they want material evidence of God, they need to survey the material extent of the universe before claiming He does not exist. And omnipresent, omniscient, and omnipotent are attributes usually given to God; therefore, it takes a God to say that there is no God. But we are mere mortals dwelling on a speck of dust in this vast cosmos.

Atheism has to wait forever to conclude that God does not exist since the chain of cause and effect lapses into *reductio ad absurdum* in their reductionist worldview. Furthermore, how does one know that science will never discover evidence of God when it probes into the origins of the universe and our consciousness? Atheism is not only unscientific and irrational but is also against the very spirit of scientific enquiry.

PRINCIPLE OBJECTIONS OF THE ATHEISTS

So far, we have seen how unscientific and irrational atheism is. In this chapter, we will point out that there is incoherence even in the objections they raise against theism. The militant atheists who base their worldview on scientific materialism think philosophy and theology are useless and yet ironically go on to raise philosophical and theological objections for the existence of God. Philosophical objections like celestial teapots, god-of-the-gaps, Occam's razor, and theological ones like the problem of suffering are a few they bring up often in debates.

Few atheists also claim that the "why" questions are irrelevant, yet go on to disbelieve precisely because they are not satisfied with our answers to their own set of whimsical "why" questions. Their favourite one is "Why is there suffering and evil in the world?" One of the four cowboys of militant atheism, Sam Harris asks another such whimsical question: "Why the universe is so large and wasteful?"

We have to remember that none of these are scientific or rational questions and therefore cannot have scientific or rational answers. We will show why they cannot be scientific or rational later in the chapter, but suffice it to say now that none of these objections can be used to justify atheism in a scientific journal or peer reviewed scientific paper.

We will deal with the first set of objections that every atheist comes up in debates: the onus of proof, lack of evidence, and god-of-the-gaps. All three are interrelated and at times overlap.

One of the most common strategies of the militant atheists is to push the onus of proof on the theists. Really? Did they expect us to go back in time with a digicam and record God in the act of creation? Or bring a signed note from Jesus with the message "I am the Son of God?" How can two pugilists decide what exists or not in the entire cosmos by arm-wrestling with each other in their local pub? How intellectually Ptolemaic can one get? Our knowledge is but a drop in an ocean of ignorance and what exists out there is independent of what we can prove to each other. And how convenient, push the onus of proof on the theists and swing in a hammock under a tree. Is this a way to decide the answer to the most important question for humanity?

For a moment let us switch places. What evidence do they have for abiogenesis? The belief that life arose randomly out of chemical slime? None whatsoever. And how do they propose to bring about the universe? Out of nothing? Really? Clearly, the onus of proof is on both sides.

When confronted with questions that they cannot answer, they will blame the theists for resorting to the god-of-the-gaps. Another lazy excuse we will deal with a little later. What we should remember here is that no scientist will push the hypothesis of abiogenesis and use such lame philosophical excuses when asked to present the evidence. Why then bring it up here? Einstein once remarked that no amount of experimentation can prove a theory right, but a single experiment can prove it wrong. How then do they know that the gap in question will not overturn a materialistic explanation of the origin of life and make atheism untenable?

The very fact that scientists are trying hard in their laboratories to create artificial life is in itself QED for intelligent causation. And so is fine-tuning of the laws of physics. What more proof do they want? God Himself to descend and shake their hands? Or perhaps the angels in their legions to sing a lullaby to them? If they are not convinced by the astounding power, order, and wisdom found in nature then even if angels come down they will not believe. Instead they will delude themselves into thinking that they are some friendly aliens from outer space!

"Lack of evidence" is another excuse which is also invalid. As pointed out earlier, claiming there is "lack of evidence" is not the same as saying "we don't know." The former is implying that one knows everything, but see no evidence of God, while the latter is admitting that one still doesn't know enough to decide. To note this difference is crucial, especially since we currently don't know everything about the cosmos. To say that there is no evidence for God in the universe when our knowledge of its origin is incomplete is speaking too soon.

Such excuses are therefore inadmissible in the court of law. Instead they will be admonished for being lazy and will be advised to return after the investigation is complete. They should instead be saying "We don't know," and confess that they are ignoramuses. To say that there is a lack of evidence and placing the onus on believers is a convenient cop out.

Let us again switch places for a moment—what evidence does NASA have for aliens? How come they are spending millions of dollars to search for alien life on Mars despite not having a shred of evidence? Why such colossal waste of money while millions in Africa are dying of starvation? Scientists in NASA would have surely done better if they had taken lessons on compassion from Christianity before they spent public money away in such futile pursuits. If they think that we believe in the myths of the past, they are no better in blindly believing the modern-day myths like Star Trek, Star Wars, and War of the Worlds. God help us from the generation that was brought up watching such scientific myths on their idiot boxes.

Resorting to the god-of-the-gaps excuse may have worked when theists were appealing to mystery not too long ago. The atheists are pretty outdated on this front, the debate has moved on long ago. We are no longer pointing to some mystery, but are pointing to empirical evidence of complexity found in nature. The complexity of the cell and the fine-tuning of the laws of physics are a few examples. The god-of-the-gaps excuse is invalid in such cases.

More importantly, the origin of the universe, of matter and the laws of physics, of life, and of consciousness are anything but minor gaps. These are fundamental questions of existence that atheism needs to answer. If they think that these are some minor gaps that science will provide answers for one day, then they are deluding themselves. Science can never help atheism in answering the origin of the universe question because of its causal methodology. Every effect must have a cause. Science will inevitably relapse into *reductio ad absurdum ad infinitum.*

Perhaps one of the most common fallacies that atheists resort to is that if science can provide explanations, then they think there is no need to invoke God. We will deal with this fallacy later in the chapter on science. But to answer this briefly, every roadside mechanic can explain how an automobile engine works in purely physicochemical terms, but that does not mean Ford doesn't exist. This is a *non sequitur.* Scientific explanation in no way implies the non-existence of God.

Give a toddler a set of Lego blocks, with some space and unlimited time in her crèche, she will more or less figure out all the permutations and combinations that are possible. What is so great about science when it does exactly what the toddler is doing? The real question for the atheists then is: where on earth or in the universe are they going to get the dimensions of space and time along with matter and forces that govern it from? Until science has answered this fundamental question, it has answered nothing. We have already noted that the very method of science—causality—disallows any such ultimate answers. That the universe exists is itself the greatest of all wonders.

We will briefly deal with two other common objections and move on. One is to point to bad designs found in nature and ridicule God. The other is to try and give a materialistic explanation (evolutionary or genetic) for religious belief and then go on to dismiss them as irrational by-products of evolution or of their genome. Both of these atheistic arguments are self-defeating and self-contradictory.

There are four reasons why a few bad designs found in nature do not negate intelligent causation. Firstly, it is a statistical no-brainer. For every supposed bad design, we can point to a hundred brilliant designs and win hands down. Secondly, it is more rational for us to believe that the less optimized designs are a result of low priority than to believe that the highly optimized ones came about by sheer dumb luck of random mutations.

Thirdly, if I were an engineer who could make a robot which possesses such great intelligence that it could optimize and improve its own functionality then I would be considered an extraordinary genius. Ditto for the design of humans by God. By pointing to a few designs that could be better, they have just increased my respect for the brilliant design of my brain which spotted them in the first place. And this is inversely proportional: the more I can improvise, the more I admire my well-designed brain!

Lastly, it is a self-defeating argument. If bad design is evidence for God's non-existence then our brain must also have been formed by some unguided random processes and therefore all its conclusions need to be thrown out of the window, including the conclusion of bad design. Not only that, they should be sceptical of their atheism as well.

Richard Dawkins mocks intelligent causation by pointing to the extra length of laryngeal nerve of a giraffe. For us, it is like a person going into a complex data centre (the brain is the most complex entity in the entire known universe) and looking at all the complicated networks, switches, routers, and firewalls and come out thinking "It could not have been designed," just because he saw an extra cable somewhere. This is being petty to the power of infinity.

Another flawed argument of the atheists is to trace the origin of our belief in evolution, in our genes, or in the chemicals of our body. By doing this, they claim that belief is not rationally derived, but is rather a by-product of evolution, or of a particular configuration of the brain, or the result of a particular stew of chemicals in our head. The funny thing is that they trace religious belief to a materialistic or evolutionary cause and yet somehow assume they are transcendent mutants who have risen above evolution and chemicals. If they think I am a believer because I have excess of "theistocin" in my brain then maybe its deficiency is what makes one an atheist. Perhaps they have an excess of another chemical called "atheistoxin" which makes them atheistic. Maybe evolution wants to do away with the monogamy of Christianity so that one can spawn their genes without limiting to one partner. Where is the objectivity in science and rationality here? Unless of course, they think they are some transcendent super-intellects whose rational deductions are beyond the influence of chemicals residing in their brains. We will have nothing to do with such elitist snobbery.

Coming to their whimsical "why" questions, we confess that we have no pretensions of knowing all the answers to their questions, but we know out of experience that no answer we give will ever satisfy these eternal pessimists because of their bias. At the same time, we are confident that no answer can ever nullify the other powerful evidence of God that we already have in context of the creation of our cosmos and life.

As mentioned earlier, the "why" questions cannot be either scientific or rational. They cannot be scientific because the scientists themselves term such questions irrelevant. We must accept the phenomena as it is and not how we whimsically want it to be. If they don't like the nature of God as revealed in the Bible, then that is still no reason to deny His existence.

They cannot be rational because one cannot answer questions of a given rational framework in an entirely different one. For example, one cannot ask Christianity to rationalize the Epicurean concepts of well-being. In mathematics, no one applies the rules of set theory to do trigonometry.

One of their favourite "why" questions is the problem of suffering. With this, they subtly appeal to emotions rather than the intellect of the audience. They ask the audience how a good God can allow such pain and suffering that we see in the world. For us, this is a theological question that has been answered two millennia ago by the Apostles and the early church fathers who experienced more suffering and persecution than can be imagined in the present world. But if those theological answers do not satisfy the atheists, then they should not be asking such theological questions in the first place. On one hand, the atheists refuse to see any value in theology, yet go on to point to a common misunderstanding about suffering and assume it can never be answered.

Even if the atheists do not see the evidence of a "good" God, it still cannot be an excuse for unbelief. It is a complete *non sequitur* to disbelieve in a noun just because one doubts the adjective. This is another fallacy we have to do away with. No one in his right mind will say Jesus does not exist just because they don't like what He said or did. In the same way, no one rejects the force of gravity because he was hurt when an apple plonked on his head or he broke a bone when he fell off a tree. In science, we accept the phenomena as it is and not how we whimsically want it to be. Ditto with God. Emotional responses should not get in the way of truth. Instead, the debate can now focus on the nature of God rather than on the existence of God.

And if they are rejecting the existence of a "good" God then how do they know that He is not good in the first place? We have already pointed out that the only way of knowing a person's mind is via revelation. God has revealed Himself to be a compassionate God in many passages of the Bible (Jeremiah 9:23-24) and also by laying down His very life for humanity. But the atheists seem to think that they are some super psychologists who know God more than He knows Himself! The howl of the Rottweiler is a textbook example of this hubris (See *The God Delusion*, chapter two, first para.) Such strident conclusions of the atheists on the nature of God are absurd and unwarranted. Terry Eagleton reviewing *The God Delusion* had this to say: "Imagine someone holding forth on biology whose only knowledge of the subject is the Book of British Birds, and you have a rough idea of what it feels like to read Richard Dawkins on theology."

It is also wrong to assume that life was meant to be a pleasure trip. It is not. It is rather a dispensation of grace given for repentance. In the Christian worldview, the suffering in this world and the dismal state of nature is exactly what one would expect to see when the creation has been banished from the presence of God. We are a brilliant creation that has fallen. The whim of atheists to have only pleasure and no pain is totally irrelevant to the existence of God. In this context, we see no difference between a Islamic jihadi and an atheist. The former is accepting God for the promised pleasure of meeting seventy-two virgins in the afterlife while the latter is rejecting God because he is denied that pleasure in this life itself!

If atheists are still not convinced with our answers to the problem of evil and suffering and claim that it is an irresolvable problem for theism then we would like to remind them that there are irresolvable problems in every other rational framework as well. In fact, there are irresolvable problems even in science too. There are many unanswered questions both in science and theism. If it is god-of-the-gaps then it could also be atheism-of-the-gaps. Why be optimistic in one and be pessimistic in the other? How come the lack of evidence for abiogenesis is seen as god-of-the-gaps while the lack of evidence for Abraham is seen as a confirmation of his absence? Why is my confidence in the existence of God seen as "faith" while the blind faith of scientists in abiogenesis and multiverse is called "confidence?" Why these double standards?

Many atheistic philosophers bring up incompatibility arguments against the nature of God using comic trivializations. Epicurus thought he was so smart to point out that God could not be both Omnipotent and Omnibenevolent because evil exists in the world. It may have been okay for Greeks to bring up such lazy arguments sitting on the shores of the idyllic Mediterranean, but the modern philosophers have no excuse to blindly mimic them. In quantum physics, the position of an electron can be here and there and everywhere whether the atheists are able to rationalize it or not. Reality as we currently know it, is stranger than fiction. If an electron can be everywhere at the same time then why cannot God be both Omnipotent and Omnibenevolent at the same time? Before making grandiose claims on God's nature, why not put to test the atheistic worldview itself right at the outset? In an atheistic worldview, we are nothing but physics and chemistry and our free will is an illusion. In which case, there can be no objective analysis of anything. All our rationality is an illusion and that should include the incompatibility argument against God's nature. "For the wisdom of this world is foolishness with God. For it is written, He taketh the wise in their own craftiness." (I Corinthians 3:19.)

The last objection we will deal with is also the most trivial. Lawrence Krauss thinks that God explains nothing. We don't think so. In fact, we think God explains infinitely more than "nothing," which the atheistic shenanigans believe that everything came out of. God indeed explains where the incredible power, order, and wisdom that is needed to create a universe like ours came from.

Key Summary

Many atheists claim that theology, philosophy, and the "why" questions in life are pointless, yet go on to disbelieve precisely for those reasons. Celestial teapots, theodicy, and "why is there evil in this world?" are a few examples which we have answered in this chapter.

The only "rational" objections they have is the lack of evidence, onus of proof, and god-of-the-gaps. One cannot claim that there is "lack of evidence" while having half knowledge—especially when we have no clue about the origins of our universe and life. This is inadmissible in the judicial courts. It is also unfair to push the "onus of proof" on the believers and sit back. Two pugilists cannot decide what exists or not by arm-wrestling in their local pub. Lastly, theists are no longer pointing to gaps in knowledge to claim the existence of God. They are instead pointing to incontrovertible evidence of intelligent causation from what we know—the intricate structure of a living cell.

The why questions always tend to be whimsical. We have no pretensions of knowing all the answers to every "why" question that atheists ask and no answer we give them will ever convince these eternal pessimists. At the same time, we are very sure that no answer can negate the other powerful evidence we have for God's existence.

The "why" questions are neither scientific nor rational questions and therefore cannot have scientific and rational answers. It is unscientific because we have to accept the phenomena as it is and not how we whimsically want it to be. It is irrational because we cannot rationalize Christian concepts in an Epicurean framework. No one uses set theory to do trigonometry.

The problem of suffering has always been raised by the atheists in debates. There is no reason to believe that this universe was meant to be a pleasure trip. In a Christian worldview, we are a fallen creation that have been given a dispensation of grace to repent and return to God.

If atheists are not convinced with the answers we have given to various objections that they have raised and think that these are irresolvable problems of theism then we would like to remind them that there are irresolvable problems in every other rational framework as well. In fact, there are irresolvable problems even in science too. There are many unanswered questions both in science and theism. If it is god-of-the-gaps then it could also be atheism-of-the-gaps. Why be optimistic in one and pessimistic in the other?

WHAT HAS SCIENCE GOT TO
DO WITH ATHEISM?

Nothing. *Rien. Nada. Niets. Ingenting. Nichts. Kuch bhi nahin.* Absolutely nothing! It is baffling to see the atheists give endless homilies on science and its methodology which is pointless to this debate. Their books are more about science than atheism. Everyone agrees that the scientific method is a great way of unravelling nature within certain definite limits. No one is denying that, not even the theists. In fact, science has enabled me to have a grander perspective of God and has infinitely increased my conviction. Even many pioneers of science like Newton and Faraday were firm believers of God which shows that science has nothing to do with atheism. In this short chapter, we will once and for all sever any ties that the atheists imagine there is between science and atheism. Once we do that, the poverty of their worldview will become abundantly clear.

We have already seen in the previous chapter that it is impossible to deny the existence of ETI or God while having half knowledge about the universe. On the contrary, we can affirm their existence with limited knowledge. We have plenty of positive evidence to prove that God exists, which we have articulated in the first chapter. The signature of intelligent causation in the living cell is also unmistakable. If the evidence presented does not convince the atheists, they still have no right to be atheistic while having incomplete knowledge about our universe.

We hear the atheists say quite often that science is enough, and that they have no need of God. Enough for what? Science is a puerile commentary of nature. *It is merely discovering how the universe works and not inventing it.* This observation is key. By discovering and labelling the laws and forces that govern it, we are simply correlating data and deducing equations that correspond to reality. But the central question that atheists have to answer is the genesis question. Pointing to puerile mathematical equations will not suffice. They are after-the-fact descriptions of reality and not some abracadabra spell that will conjure up a universe out of nothing.

What science can do effectively is to enable us to understand nature by taking certain entities for granted as its axioms and postulates. For example, given the atomic particles and the forces that govern them, we can comprehend how all the elements of the universe came to be and how they interact with each other. But what is so great about that? If we give a toddler a bunch of Lego blocks that have predefined shapes and rules of assembling plus ample space in her crèche and unlimited time to play around, she will eventually figure out all the permutations and combinations that are possible. The real question for science and atheism is: where are they going to get those Lego blocks with predefined rules, space, and time from?

Scientists are simply taking for granted what they see in nature—energy, matter, and the laws that govern our universe. It is funny to see the discoverer applauded and given all sorts of Nobel Prizes while the inventor is left out. In fact, it is even funnier to see laws of nature named after their discoverers (like Newton's laws and Boyle's laws) rather than after the inventor. This is a typical colonial attitude that we have to do away with in science. "… knowledge puffeth up…" (1 Corinthians 8:1.)

While the applied sciences can go about their business by simply taking for granted all the energy, matter, and the laws that govern them, the atheists cannot afford to do that. The real question for the atheist then is not how the universe works, but how it came to be in the first place. Where did the axioms and postulates of science: matter and the laws that govern it come from? Atheism must begin with nothing—absolutely nothing—and explain how everything including us, came about. But all we hear from the atheistic camp is a deafening silence. *Ex nihilio nihil fit* (Out of nothing comes nothing.)

Science cannot bail out atheism here. We have already pointed out that the origins question is forever beyond the scope of reductionist science. Every equation in science must have entities on the left as well as the right-hand side. This denotes causality which is one of the pillars of the scientific methodology. Every effect must have a cause. The mother of all questions then is what caused the universe? And what caused the cause of the universe? Science is clearly doomed to be an ignoramus forever about the origin of the cosmos.

It is true that the same question can be asked of God as well but it should be clear to us by now that there are no rational or scientific answers to this question. It is a miracle that the cosmos exists and the origins question will have the same two preternatural solutions—we were either created by an entity that could create itself or by an eternally existing entity. Whatever science labels that entity, we revere that entity as our Creator God without whom we would not be here.

Even if scientists are not convinced theists, they cannot escape being deists or pantheists. One must postulate a God-like being—a self-creating (or eternally existing) omnipotent, omnipresent, and omniscient entity—to account for the incredible power, order, and wisdom that we see in the cosmos and in living systems. Even if scientists are unwilling to accept anything beyond what they observe or rationally deduce, they cannot avoid being pantheists. For them, studying nature is equivalent to studying God and doing science is doing theology.

It is truly a wonder that we can do science in the first place. It takes two miracles to do science: a universal order and a free conscious mind. It is remarkable that there is universal order in nature. Every electron that is formed anywhere in the universe knows the exact parameters it should possess. Without this universal order, scientists would have been jobless cobblers.

A free conscious mind is also a must for our science to be objective. Without free will, objective science is illusory. No amount of sophistry from the atheistic camp can bail them out here.

We are not only fortunate to have a universal order and a free conscious mind to do science, but are also extremely fortunate that the universe itself is amenable to scientific inquiry. In their book *The Privileged Planet: How Our Place in the Cosmos Is Designed for Discovery*, Guillermo Gonzalez and Jay Richards show us how our place in space and time is extraordinarily special. It is not only remarkably designed to bring us into existence but also to further scientific exploration.

The best of scientific evidence refutes the Copernican Principle, the widely held idea that there is nothing special about earth or its place in the universe. The earth is precisely positioned in the Milky Way not only for life to exist, but also to allow us to find answers to the greatest mysteries of the universe.

Striking facts like how water doesn't behave like most other liquids, how its quirky properties make it perfectly suited to sustain life, and how Jupiter and Saturn protect life on earth from cataclysmic destruction clearly show our privileged place in the universe. If atheists still want to insist that all of these favourable conditions came about by sheer dumb luck then we will have nothing to do with such cosmic punters.

Some atheists conveniently turn this argument upside down and claim that we would not be here if the universe were not supportive of life and therefore there is nothing special about it. This is a convenient cop out. It is like a passenger in a train refusing to pay for the ticket since the train was heading to his destination anyway! It is very unlikely that the ticket inspector will nod at the passenger's wisdom and move on.

We may be here because of the way our universe has been in the past, but it did not need to support life in the very next second. It could have blown us to smithereens in the next second. We may be in a universe that can sustain life but not in one that can create it since we still have no clue how life came to be in the first place. We may be in the universe that can sustain life but it did not have to create intelligent life which would ponder on it. Or create such spellbinding and beautiful innovations that we find in nature. All these cry out for an explanation.

Atheism not only has nothing to do with science, but is also in direct contradiction to its method. While scientists concern themselves with order that is found in nature and establish causal relationships, atheists constantly appeal to nothingness and randomness, both of which are exact opposites of the scientific methodology. While "nothing" breaks causality which is one of the sacred pillars of science, terms like random, fluke, and chance are mere English words devoid of any meaning in science. By doing that, the atheists are on a collision course with the scientific method.

Atheism is also against the very spirit of science for another reason. Even if the evidence presented by the theists does not satisfy them, how do they know for certain that future science will never find incontrovertible proof for the existence of God? Science changes every day as new data pours in. It is a very dynamic discipline. Our understanding of the cosmos constantly varies. Existing theories could be uprooted and replaced by new ones. How then do they know that future science will never discover the existence of God? Unless of course they are claiming to be soothsayers of scientism.

Apart from all the above contradictions between science and atheism, one really stands out. If there is a scenario where our endeavor to understand nature through science should be suspect, it is in the atheistic worldview. To the extent that if one is an atheist then one must throw all science out of the window counting it as subjective nonsense because in their worldview we are entities that are optimized for survival and nothing more. We will also have to be suspicious whether we are capable of detecting all the phenomenon there is in the universe since there might be phenomena that may not have any survival value. As an example, even though outer space appears dark, it could be teeming with phenomena which have no survival value for us. In an atheistic worldview, science cannot know what it does not know. If we are incapable of detecting all the phenomena there is, then how can we conclude with incomplete knowledge that God does not exist? To make things worse, we will also have to suspect the output of our processor—the brain—since they claim that it has not been designed to do objective science or to think rationally, but for ruthless survival. And if our mind is "nothing but" the brain then free will is an illusion and objective science a myth.

Atheists like Stephen Hawkins, Richard Dawkins, and Sam Harris usually demean humanity by calling them chemical scum, lumbering robots, stuff of yeast, and so on. But why will anyone then believe the same chemical scum if it goes on to make grandiose statements that there is no God? In such a scenario, it takes immense amount of blind faith on the part of atheists to trust their own conclusions. On the contrary, it is perplexing to see atheists being all the more dogmatic about their knowledge instead of being most sceptical of it. Unless of course, they are telling us that they are some special creation who have transcended their chemistry and biology. We somehow get the feeling that they want to believe that they are made in the image of God but without God!

Finally, when the theists present empirical evidence, atheists become unduly pessimistic or resort to unverifiable speculations. A true scientist will be more confident of the brute fact at hand rather than a couple of unproven speculations in the bush. Not so in the case of atheists. Even when fine-tuning is a brute fact of nature, atheists try to circumvent it by resorting to unverifiable speculations like the string landscape or inflationary universes. Conversely, abiogenesis has been continuously falsified both in nature and in the laboratory for more than a century, yet they have blind faith that life formed by fluke in a chemical broth. When it comes to presenting evidence, atheists conveniently depart from brute facts of science and resort to speculative imaginations or unacceptable assertions.

It is baffling to see Richard Dawkins who professes to be a strong promoter of science supporting hypotheses that have no empirical evidence. A universe out of nothing and abiogenesis are the two atheistic delusions that he supports without batting an eyelid. To use his own words: what logic, observation, and evidence does he have to prove abiogenesis or that a universe can pop out of absolutely nothing? For anyone who cares to notice, it should be abundantly clear as to who the true enemy of reason is.

Many atheists claim that majority of the scientists do not believe in God. But who cares? We are more interested in what they can empirically prove or rationally deduce rather than what they "believe." It is not as though they have done a deep scientific and rational analysis to conclude that God does not exist. When we probe deeper as to why they don't believe, most of them usually give vague reasons for not believing (my daughter died in an accident, therefore God does not exist), or are too busy to think about such questions, or have some hidden philosophical bias, or simply don't care about such deeper questions. Some are even fearful of losing their academic positions if they confess their faith. Such polls are therefore inconsequential to this debate. In cases when the voters themselves are confused, truth cannot be decided by a Gallup poll.

Few important conclusions should be plain to us by now. First and foremost, science has absolutely no business with atheism. Secondly, atheism is against the very spirit of science because it always appeals to nothingness and random chance and has blind faith that science will never discover further evidence of God in the future. Thirdly, in an atheistic and materialistic worldview, science can never be trusted since they believe it to be a product survival machines which cannot even in principle have free will. In fact, the atheistic worldview makes "objective science" untenable. Objective science can only be possible in a theistic worldview. And finally, the atheists become Holocaust deniers when presented with empirical evidence for the existence of God and resort to unverifiable claims and speculations which are utterly unscientific and irrational. Science and atheism therefore can never be brothers-in-arms.

Key Summary

Science has no business with atheism, yet the atheists continue to use science as a red herring in all their books and debates. Just because science explains something does not mean that God does not exist. Every road-side mechanic knows how an automobile engine works but that in no way means Ford does not exist. This is *non sequitur.*

Science is puerile commentary. It is discovering how the universe works and not inventing it. Science simply takes matter and the laws that govern it for granted. Give a toddler a bunch of Lego blocks and the space of her crèche with unlimited time, she will more or less figure out all the permutations and combinations. What is so great about science when it is doing precisely what the toddler is doing? The real question for atheists is where is science going to get matter, space, and time from?

Ironically, the atheists believe that the universe came out of nothing, that the laws are inherent to nature, and the fine-tuning was sheer dumb luck. None of these are scientific or rational. They are atheistic assertions that we firmly reject.

LIMITS OF SCIENCE

The militant atheists always appeal to science and its methodology in their books and debates but they hardly ever mention its limits. They conveniently ignore questions that are more fundamental than the ones science can answer. Scientific materialism therefore needs a reality check. We need to probe what it can rationally explore, what is beyond its scope, and the hidden assumptions that it takes for granted. Their dogmatic epistemological claims need to be questioned and examined carefully. If we ever need to have a questioning mind, it is here. When we do that, we can clearly see the humbling limits of science. We will examine a few crucial and fundamental limits of science in the paragraphs that follow.

Firstly, science is as much a divine revelation as religion. Unless the phenomenon reveals itself to us, we would have no clue about its existence. Unfortunately, nature has been a miser in revealing only five percent of itself to us so far. The rest of the ninety-five percent has been labeled by scientists as dark matter and energy. The word "dark" here being a substitute for "we have no clue."

This is a startling realization of cosmology. The universe seems to hold more matter and energy than can be detected by our instruments. And until nature reveals that portion to us we will never know what dark matter and energy is. In this scenario, we have at least deduced that we are in the dark, but there could be phenomena that we have absolutely no clue about. Science cannot know what it does not know. If one thinks that nothing can exist beyond what we as humans can detect or deduce, then that is a fine example of intellectual solipsism.

It is also divine revelation if we remove free will and denigrate consciousness as a *post facto* irrelevant sensation of the brain. If we have no clue on how our brain works then how can we trust what pops out of it as a revelation to our consciousness? Including some of the highly speculative cosmological theories that are beyond empirical verification?

Viewed this way, there is no difference between science and religion. Both are quests for truth. Both are revelation based. One seeks to understand the material world through revelation and the other seeks to understand the mind of God through revelation.

There is then no conflict between science and religion since both are revelations of God. One revelation is about His creation and the other about His mind and purpose. There can be no dichotomy between them. Almost all the pioneers of science like Newton and Faraday believed that nature revealed the glory of God. The militant atheists should perhaps heed to what their own poster boy Galileo Galilei had to say about science and religion: "The Bible shows the way to go to heaven, not the way the heavens go."

Secondly, science may be objective but it is also subjective to its practitioners and the sensors they have. It is also subjective to the processing powers of its practitioners as well. Humans have a few inbuilt sensors like eyes for sight, ears for sound, nose for smell, and skin for sensation. We can happily correlate information about them until kingdom come, but it would in no way mean that is all there is to the universe. There can be no objective truths in science, only those which are subjective to its practitioners and the sensors that they possess.

Consider the parable of the digicams. Two digital cameras with light sensors will agree on everything they detect but are strictly limited to speak, theorize, and debate about light waves only. Now suppose a new digital camera is developed which has sensors to detect the dimension of time and sound, which we call a video camera. The other two might scorn the new kid on the block and think it is deluded to hear sounds and experience the extra dimension of time, whatever those are supposed to be. They may even smartly shift the onus on the video camera to prove that something called "sound" exists. But unfortunately, the video camera may not have a processor which is smart enough to prove it to others via a debate. It merely has a sound detecting device and a processor to report and analyse that sound. Fortunately, the video camera will become more popular because of these new features while the other two will end up in the scrap heap.

Put spiritual experience in place of sound and you will know what we mean. As pointed out in the last chapter, atheism is not only unscientific but it is also against the very spirit of scientific enquiry. It is hypocritical of the atheists to be sceptical of one spiritual dimension—for which empirical evidence exists in the form of near-death experiences recorded everywhere in the world by medical sciences—while happily assuming seven more dimensions to justify string theory and its infinite landscape even when they don't have an iota of evidence to present. By the way, physicists are mathematically conjuring up seven more dimensions just to cover up the most embarrassing situation that prevails in the physics department—their inability to unify quantum physics with general relativity.

There are empirical facts that are currently unable to correlate to any theoretical framework and there are speculative theories that are yet to ascertain empirical evidence. There are also many natural phenomena like consciousness that cannot be empirically detected and many empirical phenomena like quantum entanglement that are anything but "rational." Given a choice between empirical data that has not been understood and a puerile speculative theory that has no empirical data, one should err on the side of empirical data even if it cannot be rationalized currently.

Spiritual experiences are precisely the empirical phenomena that we need to look at carefully. Many scientists claim that these experiences are delusions. How can they assume that? For a digital camera without sound sensors, sound will seem to be a delusion. But is it? How do they know that there is no spiritual dimension out there waiting to be discovered?

Thirdly, quantum physics is not science but the end thereof. The two sacrosanct pillars of science—causality and objectivity—have been blown to smithereens in the quantum world. The quantum phenomenon therefore is anything but "natural." Many students get utterly disappointed after they study quantum physics and understandably so. In the quantum world, even the objective nature of reality is in question. It is amusing to see the atheists use the weird and preternatural quantum phenomenon to conjure up our universe out of nothing, all the while blissfully ignoring its implications. It may shock many to know that in the quantum world, it takes an observer to actuate a subatomic event. There can be no independent reality without an observer. Since the big bang was also a quantum event to begin with, who was the observer at that point of time? These are hard questions that atheists must answer.

Fourthly, the atheists proudly claim that there is no Islamic or Christian Science, forgetting that chemistry was once called alchemy and their astronomy was once called astrology. Science may not vary in the dimension of space (or geography) but it does vary tremendously in the dimension of time. Science was very different before the theory of relativity and got even stranger after quantum physics. What is the guarantee then, that the present knowledge is conclusive? If there are no absolute truths in science, then even atheism that is based on it is a fluid concept. Who knows what is in store tomorrow? Nowhere are the atheists committing a greater blunder than jumping to conclusions while having incomplete knowledge about the origin of our cosmos and life.

Besides, why are the atheists taking the credit for a unified science? This is not a greatness of science but the incredible consistency of the laws of nature found in the universe. Matter and forces of nature are universally consistent as far as we can tell. Imagine the pandemonium if every electron in existence had a different mass and charge. Scientists would have been jobless cobblers if it were not for this incredible condition of the universe. We don't see why they should be boasting about this.

Fifthly, our science is also terribly parochial in space and time considering the extent of the cosmos and the time that has elapsed since the creation. We can only speculate and deduce what happened in the past but there is no way we can be sure of our conclusions. And no telling what is going on in galaxies so far away that it appears as a faint blob even in the best telescopes of today.

Sixthly, science currently has no tools to detect consciousness, forget about understanding it. How then does it propose to detect the mind of God? If scientists cannot even tell what I am thinking, how do they propose to know what is on God's mind? As mentioned earlier, in a theistic worldview, God is not a thing but a person and it is His prerogative to reveal Himself to whomsoever He wishes—His saints and prophets—and not to every tom, dick, and harry in the science department.

In science, the phenomenon will decide how it can be detected and not the lazy atheists sitting in their veranda and issuing a *habeas corpus* to God. If the quantum nature of reality can be so counterintuitive that it takes a paradigm shift to understand it then why not a paradigm shift on the methods to detect God? The methodology for detecting God could be completely unconventional and different. It is clear through the scriptures that it takes not only knowledge but also character to detect Him. "…holiness, without which no man shall see the Lord:" (Hebrews 12:14.) Only minds that are in a holy and pure state can detect the phenomenon called God. It took decades to prepare the Large Hadron Collider (LHC) for detecting Higgs, in the same way it takes a lifetime of preparation to reach a state when we can commune with God.

Seventhly, science has no provision for assuming speculations to be true. They will remain speculations until proven. If one wants to bank on those speculations then one does so out of blind faith. Unfortunately, scientific materialists have as much faith if not more than theists, but subtly choose to call it "confidence." The scientists at CERN *(European Organization for Nuclear Research)* had no clue if Higgs Boson existed or not. They only had "faith" in the standard model of nuclear physics. They went on to spend billions of dollars building the LHC based on it. What a waste of resources it would have been if they had not found the Higgs particle. Sadly, not all scientific missions have been that successful. NASA has already wasted millions of dollars in trying to find life on Mars where none exists.

Eighthly, scientific knowledge is ephemeral. It is continuously changing as new discoveries are made. In a reductionist world, they will be forever learning because causality will never allow them to rest. If the quarks and electrons are currently accepted as the fundamental constituents of matter, the next generation will ask where did the parameters that define them come from? The current fad is strings, but future generations will ask how did the strings get the parameters that define them? And the story will go on forever.

Before we end this chapter, we must put an end to the myth that all scientific exploration is unbiased. Everyone speaks about Galileo Galilee but seemed to have forgotten Ludwig Boltzmann. Galileo is the poster boy of every atheist who conveniently forgets what dogmatic science has done to countless scientists who were ridiculed for their ideas initially but were later vindicated by research. Boltzmann's thesis was rejected outright because it required atomic particles and during that time it was against the scientific paradigm of the day (since the wave theory was dogma in the early 1900s.) This deeply depressed Boltzmann because it would mean that his kinetic theory and statistical interpretation of the second law of thermodynamics would have to be discarded. He went on to commit suicide while holidaying with his family—a grim reminder of what dogmatic science can do to brilliant minds. The theory of evolution immediately comes to one's mind.

We can see many more such examples of bias in science. One only needs to see how Dawkins reacted to books like *Shattering the myths of Darwinism* by Richard Milton. Or more recently, we can see how P. Z. Myers and Jerry Coyne reacted to *The Science Delusion* written by Rupert Sheldrake and to the subsequent TED talk he gave—going to the extent of influencing TED to take it off their official website. On one hand, they say we should question everything and on the other react in the most insecure manner when the theory of evolution is questioned. A textbook case of double standards.

The atheists give us endless homilies on science, yet believe absurd propositions that the universe popped out of absolutely nothing, and that they can create life by introducing electric sparks into a soup of chemicals. If Islamic fundamentalism is unacceptable then even the materialistic fundamentalism of modern-day universities should be unacceptable. The scientific materialists in the universities continue to have blind faith that the origin of the universe cannot be supernatural in spite of where the evidence is pointing to. They have blind faith that life arose by a fortuitous concourse of atoms in spite of it being falsified in nature and in the laboratories for more than a century. They continue to believe that the "hard problem" of consciousness is explicable in terms of brain activity even while having no clue how the brain itself functions. How long will they deny the truth and mislead humanity by insisting on their materialistic dogma? We protested earlier when Catholicism departed from the truth, and we protest again when the current universities are doing the same with their reductionist dogma.

There are many atheists who have the audacity to say that if science cannot answer a given question, then that question is essentially meaningless. This is a dangerous predicament. We still cannot scientifically answer how the qualia of pain occurs in sentient beings, but it would be appalling to say that it is a meaningless question. There are still many questions in nature that are beyond current science: origin of the cosmos and life, quantum physics, chaotic systems, morphogenesis, consciousness, and human behavior. To deem all of these meaningless is to deem existence itself meaningless.

Before we move on, it is quite annoying to note that many atheists boast that structures like the LHC at Geneva are the modern cathedrals of humanity. But pray who has benefitted by the discovery of Higgs boson? Think of the millions of dollars spent on finding life on Mars while there are millions starving in Africa. Or the colossal pharma and medical corporates, whose exorbitant pricing has put healthcare beyond the reach of third world nations. These modern cathedrals of science have not brought an iota of comfort to the poor and downtrodden. On the contrary, particle physics has brought us to the brink of destruction via the atomic bomb. These modern cathedrals are time bombs of destruction if not tempered with Christian ethics.

Modern science itself owes Christianity a huge debt. Ever wondered why modern science did not kick start in India or China, whose civilizations were older than the Greeks? Modern science in Europe started with the Christian premise of man being made in the image of God and one who has free will, together with the faith that God will reveal all the secrets of nature to His special creation. "…seek, and ye shall find; knock, and it shall be opened to you:" (Matthew 7:7.) For a detailed analysis of this one can read *The Grand Titration, Science and Society in East and West* and *Science and Civilisation in China* by Joseph Needham. Unfortunately, atheists are committing intellectual suicide by basing their deductions on scientific materialism that cannot even accommodate free will. By doing that, the scientific materialists and the atheists are once again shackling themselves in Plato's cave.

Key Summary

The militant atheists always appeal to science and its methodology in their books and debates but they hardly ever mention its limits. Scientific materialism therefore needs a reality check. When we do that, we can clearly see the humbling limits of science.

- Science is as much a divine revelation as religion
- Science may be objective, but it is subjective to its practitioners and the sensors they have
- Quantum physics is not science but the end thereof
- Science may not vary in geography but it varies in time
- Our science is terribly parochial in space and time
- Science has no tools to detect conscious entities
- There is no provision in science to assume the validity of speculations
- Scientific knowledge is ephemeral and constantly changing

Science itself can be dogmatic at times. The materialistic dogma found in the universities today needs to be questioned. The atheists tell us to question everything but when the questioning is on evolution, they react in the most insecure manner. A textbook example of double standards.

Naturalism—taking too
much for granted

Naturalism is a philosophical belief that our universe is governed by natural laws and forces, and that there is no need to postulate anything supernatural or miraculous. They believe that the laws and forces found in nature are enough to explain the structure and behavior of our universe, from the eternal past to the eternal future. The hubris of naturalism is captured well in Carl Sagan's opening line in the first chapter of his book *Cosmos*: "The Cosmos is all that is or ever was or ever will be."

Notwithstanding such grandiose statements, is naturalism sufficient and all encompassing? Can everything be explained in a naturalistic and materialistic framework? Where is the actual evidence pointing to? What are the hidden assumptions that they are taking for granted? And are they justified in doing so? In this short chapter, we will look at the hard evidence from science and show how inadequate the naturalistic worldview is in explaining the real world out there.

At the outset, we have to make a clear distinction between science (which is a method of knowing) and scientific materialism (which is a philosophical presupposition.) Unfortunately, scientific materialism has become the default position in the universities because the academia is unreasonably biased towards naturalism. If science is a sincere quest for truth then it should do away with philosophical baggage like naturalism, reductionism, and materialism. By insisting on these philosophical presuppositions, the universities of this day and age are straying away from a sincere quest for truth. No wonder that the modern-day universities in the west are churning out atheistic fundamentalists like the madrassas in the Middle East that are churning out Islamic fundamentalists. What we need is courage—to go boldly where the evidence is leading us—instead of imposing philosophical presuppositions on nature.

Before we look at the evidence, we should get rid of two common misconceptions which most atheists have about those who believe in God. They still seem to think that the theists believe in God only because of miracles, and strive to give a naturalistic explanation for the same. This is an outdated fallacy that we need to do away with. Theists these days are neither appealing to miracles, nor to a gap in knowledge, but are giving incontrovertible evidence of intelligent causation from phenomena that we can empirically observe. To quote Francis Bacon once again: "God never wrought miracles to convince atheism, because His ordinary works convince it."

Another common misconception most atheists have is that if science explains something using equations of known forces then there is no need to invoke God. This is another fallacious conclusion. As pointed out earlier, explaining how an automobile engine works does not preclude the existence of Henry Ford. This is a *non sequitur.*

Alvin Plantinga, Professor Emeritus of Philosophy at Notre Dame, in his book *Where the conflict really lies: Science, Religion, and Naturalism* has given a robust evolutionary argument against naturalism from a philosophical perspective. We have nothing more to add to that debate, but what we will do here is bring a fresh perspective to show how inadequate naturalism is in explaining the existence of our universe.

We have already noted that every rational framework takes certain unprovable or irreducible axioms and postulates for granted. Physicists take matter and the laws that govern it for granted. Biologists take self-replicating organisms for granted. Mathematicians take certain axioms and postulates as self-evident truth. Moral realists assume that objective morals are out there to be discovered. But the crucial question for all of them is: where on earth—or in the universe—are they getting their respective axioms and postulates from in the first place? No one has a clue about their origins. Are we not blithely taking all of them for granted? What use then, are mundane explanations when one is trying to answer fundamental questions? Ironically, they also use the miracle of consciousness and free will to claim that there are no miracles. We beg to differ from naturalism in such a scenario, and argue that nature itself is at a fundamental level preternatural.

In a reductionist worldview, there will never be an answer to the ultimate nature of things because of causality. It is sliding slope to oblivion. The naturalistic edifice then becomes a castle in the air without any foundations, and we will forever remain ignorant about the ultimate nature of reality.

Take the example of a rock which is an amalgam of various elements. These elements were cooked up in stars under high pressure and temperature. The stars themselves were formed from hydrogen and helium atoms that were created during the Big Bang. But where did the Big Bang come from? Where did matter, the laws of physics, and the constants of nature that make up the rock come from? And how are the fundamental parameters of quarks and electrons derived? Faced with such an impasse, they conveniently assume that it is inherent to the nature of things, a thing-in-itself. But how can anything be inherent, or be a "thing-in-itself" in a causal universe? In a causal universe, everything must be a derivative of something else until the physical limits of exploration are reached and we can delve no more. At which point we conveniently resign ourselves to their existence and call that phenomena "natural."

Russell Stannard in his book *The End of Discovery* says: "When it comes to understanding things-in-themselves—whether it be space, time or properties of matter—we do indeed appear to be up against a barrier of the knowable.

We do not have a language that has terms that would be capable of describing the nature of the "stuff" of a thing-in-itself."

The origin of the cosmos cannot be a natural event since we do not observe it happen in nature or in the lab. If they think that it needs special conditions that cannot be replicated, then that cannot be natural either. If they claim that it can pop out of nothing, then it is quite contradictory to the method of science to say that it is "natural" for something to come out of nothing. Instead, that statement is the very definition of a miracle! The beginning of the universe is therefore the end of science and naturalism.

If they propose that such things can happen only in the quantum world, we have already pointed out that quantum physics is not science but the end thereof. What exactly do they mean when quantum theorists tell you that the emptiness of the vacuum is seething with potentialities? There is nothing natural about that. It is clearly magical.

Coming to life itself, it is anything but natural. No one knows how life originated in the first place. We don't see it being created in warm little ponds like Darwin naively assumed. The incredible complexity of the simplest of cells is astounding and is an unmistakable signature of intelligent causation. The origin of life is so complex that even Nobel Prize winner Francis Crick confessed while researching on it that it is a miracle of sorts. The very fact that intelligent scientists are trying to figure this out is itself evidence for intelligent causation. If science has no clue how life formed then it has no right to assert that natural processes alone will suffice other than out of blind faith. Referring to historical successes of science and assuming everything can be resolved in the future is not scientific methodology either. That is not how science is supposed to work. Every day is not a Sunday.

Lastly, the phenomenon of consciousness is anything but natural. No one has a clue how to resolve the "hard problem" of consciousness. The very fact that we can think, converse, and ideate to do science is anything but natural. There may be materialistic correlates to the content of our thoughts but there are none for thought itself. The content of our consciousness is separate from the form that our consciousness takes, the atheists seem to confuse one with the other. If they still insist that the brain is the mind, then they are committing intellectual suicide. Free will in such a scenario becomes an illusion, and our science will cease to be objective.

Naturalism therefore is fundamentally flawed because nature itself has miraculous foundations. Energy and the laws of physics just popped out of nothing at the Big Bang. Around nineteen fundamental parameters of nature that are needed to make the universe are just there in nature without any reason to be. Naturalism may be okay if they are trying to explain day-to-day mundane phenomena, but it has virtually nothing to say about the deeper and more interesting questions of our existence. And if naturalism simply takes for granted all the above, then what has it explained? It is like trying to explain a successful business without having a clue where the working capital is coming from!

They are blithely taking regular miracles like these and conveniently calling them natural laws. A case in point: the speed of light is constant and no matter what speed one is travelling in, they can never catch up with the speed of light. This baffling and miraculous property was conveniently converted into an axiom by Einstein to postulate his theory of relativity!

It may be alright for scientists to assume a methodological naturalism as a working model, but to assert it in the face of contradicting evidence is to depart from truth and be dogmatic. One of the fundamental requirements of naturalism is causality. If causality breaks down then naturalism breaks down too. While we have rationally demonstrated in the above paragraphs that naturalism breaks down when it comes to the question of origins, we also have empirical evidence that naturalism breaks down even in the laboratories. Entanglement is an empirical phenomenon that continues to trouble physicists to this day. This could be that one ugly fact that destroys the beautiful assumptions of naturalism.

Naturalism not only blithely assumes the universe and its contents, but also assumes that its worldview will hold well in future explorations of the cosmos. We still have plenty to explain in nature. There are still many things we don't know about the universe. How do they know that these problems will be resolved without shaking the foundations of naturalism or current science? We already know of many beautiful theories that have been demolished by ugly facts, what guarantee that naturalism will hold in the future? Unless they are claiming to be some kind of soothsayers of naturalism who can see into the distant future.

Many believe that future technology will be indistinguishable with miracles. In which case, the Biblical miracles could be exactly that. What seems unbelievable today, may be casual tomorrow. If the naturalists do not want to believe in miracles like the theists, they should be okay to view those miracles as advanced technology. When intelligence is around, anything is possible—including virgin birth and resurrection. If they find virgin birth and resurrection ridiculous, then we find the postulates that a universe can pop out of nothing and that robots will be resurrected with consciousness someday in the future equally ridiculous.

While writing a scathing review of Carl Sagan's book *The Demon-Haunted World,* in The New York Review, Richard Lewontin writes "Our willingness to accept scientific claims that are against common sense is the key to an understanding of the real struggle between science and the supernatural. We take the side of science *in spite* of the patent absurdity of some of its constructs, *in spite* of its failure to fulfill many of its extravagant promises of health and life, *in spite* of the tolerance of the scientific community for unsubstantiated just-so stories, because we have a prior commitment, a commitment to materialism… for we cannot allow a Divine Foot in the door."

Thankfully, there are many courageous scientists and philosophers who are questioning the naturalistic and materialistic worldview in the light of emerging evidence. Thomas Nagel in his book *Mind and Cosmos* explains why the materialistic neo-Darwinian conception of nature is almost certainly false. Rupert Sheldrake in his book *The Science Delusion: Freeing the Spirit of Enquiry,* argues with clarity against the materialistic and reductionist dogma that is prevalent in the scientific community. We should encourage the scientists to free themselves from unnecessary philosophical baggage—like naturalism, reductionism, and materialism—and boldly go where the evidence is leading them. Evidence from current science already shows that naturalism is dead, but the only ones who don't seem to know about it are the naïve naturalists.

Before we move on, we have to point out that even if they insist on the naturalistic worldview, they still cannot justify atheism. Even if science does not want to speculate anything beyond the universe, they must admit that the origin of all matter and the laws that govern it—which are omnipresent and omnipotent in the universe—are fundamentally preternatural, that we are a product of a self-creating entity or an eternally existing entity. If they conveniently want to take for granted all the space-time dimensions, matter, and the laws of physics without giving any explanations then naturalism will be just another name for pantheism—the belief that God is immanent in the universe. To deny the existence of our creator is to deny the existence of the universe that created us.

Key Summary

Naturalism seems to be "familiarity breeds contempt." They are simply taking for granted what is in the universe without explaining how those came to be. We will lapse into a *reduction ad absurdum* if we dwell deeper into matter and the laws that govern it. Science has to begin with nothing and explain how everything came to be.

We currently have no clue how the universe came into existence, how the laws of nature came into existence, how the dimensions of space-time came about. We are simply taking all of these for granted. Naturalism is therefore a castle in the air without any foundations.

The origin of the universe, of life, and of consciousness are anything but natural. We still have no clue about how these came to be. The beginning of the universe therefore is the end of science and naturalism.

Is the universe rational?

Every rational organization believes that we are rational beings who can comprehend the universe. Strangely, nobody asks whether the universe itself is rational or if we humans are capable of rational thought in the first place. Since mathematics is the *lingua franca* of rationality, we assume that being rational is being mathematically consistent. If we go by this definition then the universe is anything but rational. Quantum physics blew that myth a century ago.

The greatest embarrassment for physicists is their inability to reconcile the theory of relativity with quantum physics. While the theory of relativity describes world as we see it at the macro level, quantum physics deals with the micro sub-atomic level. Both work perfectly well and are understood independent of each other. Yet both don't talk to each other. For more than a century, physicists have been struggling to reconcile them but have utterly failed.

If the reductionist approach is used for exploring nature, then it will become a *reductio ad absurdum* into nothingness. The electron is supposed to be a point particle with zero volume and the photon is supposed to have zero mass that can zoom at the fastest speed permissible. Such absurd constructs yield equations whose results are either undefined or infinite. The physicists have to resort to unwarranted procedures like "renormalizing" in order to eliminate the infinities that arise in the equations. Paul Dirac was not at all happy with this and Richard Feynman called it "hocus pocus." How then can they assume that the universe is a rational entity out there to be decoded?

Entanglement is an empirically verified irrational phenomenon. Einstein called it "spooky action at a distance," where one particle can influence the other over great distances, even if it is on the other side of the universe— in an instant, in a blink of an eye. Nobody knows how that happens and it is a direct violation of the laws of physics and causality as we currently know it. This is not some vague theoretical speculation but has been verified to be true in the laboratory.

Even within the atom, the electrons vanish from one orbit and magically appear in another orbit, this is the quantum nature of reality at the fundamental level. Nobody can tell where they are during the transition. No scientist can predict radioactive decay at the quantum level yet at the macro level its half-life is predictable. We currently have no clue how that happens and we simply cannot rationalize these situations.

What about the speed of light and our inability to attain its speed? No matter how fast we travel, we can never attain the speed of light in a vacuum. This is a cosmic speed limit that has no rational justification. It is a brute fact of reality that scientists accept and go on in life.

Perhaps the biggest blow to rationalism comes from what is called the "measurement problem" in quantum physics. Every quantum physicist knows that it takes an observer to actuate a subatomic event and until the observation occurs, reality is just a cloud of ambiguity. With this disturbing predicament arising out of the wave-particle duality of light, even the objective nature of reality is in question. No wonder Niels Bohr, the Nobel Prize winning physicist said that if one is not shocked by the quantum theory then one has not understood it. Shall we then add all the rationalist societies to this list of ignoramuses?

When one questions the physicists in the universities about this embarrassing situation in quantum physics, we are literally told to shut up and calculate. But we made the dumb machines to do exactly that. We are neither going to shut up nor are we going to mindlessly calculate. Instead, it is time for the physicists to shut up about the nature of reality.

Truth then need not be rational. It simply is, and not every truth can be rationalized. The fundamental particles of nature, quarks, and leptons are brute facts of nature whose existence cannot be rationalized. Even our consciousness cannot be rationalized in any way, it simply is the way it is. It is ironic that we use an irrational entity—our consciousness—to claim that we can rationalize everything.

As mentioned before, currently there are empirical phenomena that cannot be rationalized and rational equations that have no empirical evidence as of today. Examples are consciousness and string theory. If one has to choose to accept between empirical phenomena that have no rational explanation and a rational theory that has no empirical evidence, it is better to err on the side of the former rather than on the latter. We must believe empirical evidence irrelevant of whether it can be rationalized or not. Near-Death Experiences (NDEs) are one such phenomena which physicians throughout the world have known from people who were revived from the threshold of death. If science cannot rationalize it then that is too bad for science.

If atheists are telling us that NDEs are hallucinations, then that begs the epistemological question. If the brain is able to create such elaborate and coherent hallucinations that are experienced by those on the threshold of death, then maybe everyday reality itself is a hallucination created by the brain while we are alive. Maybe we are just a brain in a vat!

One may argue that we define reality as one that is commonly experienced by everyone. But that is forgetting other scientific methods of knowing reality which is through laboratory experiments. Not all phenomena can be detected by us in normal situations. We need certain specific conditions to detect certain phenomena. For example: we needed to construct the massive LHC to detect the Higgs particle. In the same way, maybe we need to be on the threshold of death to experience the spiritual dimensions of reality. And evidence on this front is quite strong. Even many physicians and doctors have themselves had such experiences. One such case on record is that of Eben Alexander who went on to write a book called *Proof of Heaven: A Neurosurgeons journey into the Afterlife.*

Another assumption these rationalist societies make is that man is capable of rational thought. But what are they basing their confidence on? If they are basing their view on scientific materialism then we fail to see how that could happen. The evolutionist tells you that you are "nothing but" an evolved ape, a clumsy robot designed by your genes with ruthless survival instincts. That means we are optimized for survival and not rational thought. If our conscious thought is a product of physics and chemistry, then free will is an illusion. We currently have no clue how our own brain works and are ill informed about many things in nature. What informed, rational, and objective ruminations can come out of this kind of an entity? In a materialistic worldview, objective science and rationalism are pure mythical delusions.

A free mind that can comprehend the creation of God in an "objective" way is a Christian premise but by adopting the reductionist and materialistic approach, science and rationality are together committing intellectual suicide. In their worldview, we are insignificant robots in the vastness of space and time, who are slaves of their own genomes and can have no free will. Science and rationality in such a materialistic worldview become utterly subjective, parochial, and suspect—ready to be thrown out of the window and never to be trusted again.

Before we end this chapter, we will briefly delve into mathematics, the default language of the rationalists, and see if it is enough to explore and reveal all truth. Bertrand Russell and Alfred North Whitehead with their *Principia Mathematica* set out to create one such mathematical framework which they hoped will be all encompassing. It was believed that any mathematical statement could in principle be shown to be true or false by using the axioms and postulates of their framework. That was until Kurt Gödel came along.

Kurt Gödel was a mathematical genius who firmly believed in the existence of God, and was a great friend of Albert Einstein. He came up with his "Incompleteness theorems" and proved decisively that there will always be statements of truth that cannot be proven. By doing this, he showed that any attempt to create a solid foundation for mathematics and formal systems based on a set of axioms and postulates is inherently limited. There will always be truth statements that will be unprovable. This undermines all attempts of the scientific materialists and rationalists to monopolize truth and serves as a grim reminder of the inherent limitations of all logical systems and mathematical frameworks.

While quantum physics shook the scientific materialists out of their dogmatic slumber, the Heisenberg's Uncertainty Principle and the Gödel's incompleteness theorem does the same to the rationalists who think that mathematics is all encompassing.

Key Summary

Every rational organization believes that we are rational beings who can comprehend the universe. Strangely, nobody asks whether the universe itself is rational or if we humans are capable of rational thought in the first place. Since mathematics is the *lingua franca* of rationality, we assume that being rational is being mathematically consistent. If we go by this definition then the universe is anything but rational. Quantum physics blew that myth a century ago.

Truth then need not be rational. It simply is, and not every truth can be rationalized. The fundamental particles of nature: quarks and leptons are brute facts of nature whose parameters cannot be derived in a rational way. They simply are what they are without any reason to be. Even our consciousness cannot be rationalized in any way, it simply is the way it is. It is ironic that we use an irrational entity—our consciousness—to claim that we can rationalize everything.

The rationalist societies assume that man is capable of rational thought. But what are they basing their confidence on? If they are basing their view on scientific materialism then we fail to see how that could happen. The evolutionist tells you that you are "nothing but" an evolved ape, a clumsy robot designed by your genes with ruthless survival instincts. That means we are optimized for survival and not rational thought. If our conscious thought is a product of physics and chemistry, then free will is an illusion. We currently have no clue how our own brain works and are ill informed about many things in nature. What informed, rational, and objective ruminations can come out of this kind of an entity?

A free mind that can comprehend the creation of God is a Christian premise, but by adopting the reductionist and materialistic approach, science and rationality are together committing intellectual suicide.

EVOLUTION: MUCH ADO ABOUT NOTHING

If there is one theory in science that the atheists have drawn an overdraft on to say that there is no need of God then it is the theory of evolution. This theory is the poster child of atheism. In fact, Richard Dawkins openly admits that evolution played a major role in making him an atheist. Needless to say, any book against atheism has to go head-on with this theory. And head-on it will be.

At the outset, we must do away with one fundamental misconception everyone has that evolution explains life. It simply does not. Rather it assumes and takes for granted a complex self-replicating unit of life to kick-start evolution. No one has a clue on how life originated in the first place. Absurd as it may sound, evolution needs life to explain life. No other theory in science assumes the very thing that it sets out to explain.

Whenever we confront atheists with hard questions on the origin of life they either say, "We are working on it" or blame us for invoking the god-of-the-gaps. One thing needs to be clarified here. Science, owing to its own methodology cannot force us to accept a theory on the assumption that they can demonstrate its veracity later in the future. Will atheists approve of my belief in Jesus Christ if I say that His divinity will be proven during His second advent? I am sure they will not. Then how come they expect us to do the same? We must admit with true humility that life still does not have a naturalistic explanation.

It was assumed by Darwin that life may have arisen in a warm little pond. The brute fact is that there are millions of such warm little ponds on earth, yet none of them are churning out life. Realizing this, they have now changed their minds and say that the conditions on early earth may have been different and more suitable for life to emerge. But how do they know that? This is a statement of blind faith rather than of science.

We have sent many expeditions not only to the remotest parts of the earth but also to other planets which have a myriad of conditions. But under no conditions do we see life crawling out. The focus has now shifted to the laboratories. Ironically, if scientists are trying hard in the lab to create life then that is QED for intelligent causation and not spontaneous generation. More so, when most of the methods they are using to create life are top-down rather than bottom-up. In which case, even if they succeed it simply reiterates that a conscious intelligence is needed for creating life.

If there is anything we have learned so far about the origin of life, it is the fact that physics and chemistry alone are not enough. It is not simply a question of raw materials being in the right place and at the right time. It is incredibly naive to see scientists speculate that there may be life on other planets just because certain chemicals of life were detected there. Ingredients by themselves don't give you an apple pie—you need a master chef to do the magic. A simple and elegant experiment which has been done in the laboratory clearly proves that ingredients alone are not enough. Puncture a few cells and empty all their contents into a test tube. You now have all the raw materials and components needed to make a living cell in close proximity, yet they never reassemble themselves into another cohesive living cell.

It was also thought that life was simple to start off with. In fact, it may have been so "simple" that entire generations of scientists including Nobel Prize winners have died scratching their heads to figure out the supposed simplicity. The ground reality is bad news for evolutionists—they cannot even begin to do their naturalistic science. What we currently have are speculations and motivational rhetoric which become nothing more than bestselling paperbacks. It is time we recognize all such speculations for what they are—creative imaginations of modern day alchemists. Without knowing what it takes to make life, how can we assume that random chance alone could have produced it? The onus of proof is on the atheists here.

A living cell may be physically nothing but physics and chemistry, but in its functioning, it is much more than that. It is an information processing system which can arise only by top-down design. Just like an automobile engine, we will need a meticulous assembly line to build one. We must postulate intelligence as the fifth fundamental force in the creation of life.

To quote Karl Popper, the philosopher of science, "What makes the origin of life and of the genetic code a disturbing riddle is this: the genetic code is without any biological function unless it is translated; that is, unless it leads to the synthesis of the proteins whose structure is laid down by the code. But, as Monod points out, the machinery by which the cell translates the code consists of at least fifty macromolecular components which are themselves coded in the DNA.

Thus the code cannot be translated except by using certain products of its translation. This constitutes a really baffling circle; a vicious circle, it seems, for any attempt to form a model, or theory, of the genesis of the genetic code. Thus, we may be faced with the possibility that the origin of life (like the origin of the universe) becomes an impenetrable barrier to science, and a residue to all attempts to reduce biology to chemistry and physics."

Even in the face of such overwhelming evidence of complexity and design, the atheists assert that it could have accidently assembled itself. Fred Hoyle, the English astronomer, ridiculed such naive assumptions by comparing it to a belief that a storm in a junkyard could assemble a jumbo jet by fluke. Before jump starting on evolution they have to explain how life, together with complex mechanisms like replication which are essential for evolution, came to be in the first place.

Initially, many naturalists thought that the unit of life, a prokaryote or eukaryote cell, is a featureless blob of protoplasm. No other prediction in the history of science has been more wrong than this. Even the simplest of cells is more complicated than the most intricately designed circuits of a supercomputer that man with all his intelligence can make these days. Just pick up a high school textbook of biology and see a diagram of a living cell or its micrograph and you will know what we mean. This is nanotechnology at its best. The deeper we probe, the more complicated they are turning out to be. Exactly opposite of what Peter Atkins envisages nature to be—a naive "nothing but" simplicity.

Every single cell has all the means of moving about, sustaining itself and replicating at the right time. Stephen Meyer in his book *Signature in the cell: DNA and the Evidence for Intelligent Design* clearly elucidates the amazing complexity found in the DNA and the cell in general. If you are hard pressed for time, you can watch innumerable videos made on the inner workings of a living cell on YouTube. *Secret Universe: The hidden life of the cell* by the BBC Two channel is one of the best—although it is more specific to how our cells fight viruses. And if there are videos that every family should watch in order to appreciate the complexity found in life then videos made by Illustra Media (*www.illustramedia.com*) are highly recommended.

In multicellular organisms, a single zygote has the remarkable ability to build the entire body in a process called morphogenesis, which is *the* most complex process in the known universe. It is so complex that many scientists admit that we may understand it only in the next century. If we have not understood morphogenesis then how can we assume that evolutionary mechanisms alone will be enough to bring about this complex process? Except on blind faith? The onus is again on the atheists to prove this and until they do that, they have the right to remain silent.

But the crucial point is this, if evolution cannot explain the origin of life and morphogenesis—the meticulous creation of multicellular life that happens every day and every second in the world—then what has it explained? These are crucial and fundamental questions. Evolution assumes too much and explains too little. If one were to conveniently assume the blueprint, an assembly line ready with raw materials, workers, and energy and claim to show how a car rolls out of the assemble line, then what has one explained? Evolution therefore is much ado about nothing. It is very clear that the atheists have oversold this theory in their desperation to do away with the "Divine foot."

In his book *Climbing Mount Improbable,* Richard Dawkins envisages that evolution brought about all the complexity we see in life gradually like a gentle slope of a hill. This is a myth that current evidence utterly demolishes. Right at the beginning is the origin of life, which is itself one steep slope that is impossible to scale. In fact, Mount Improbable might have the steepest slope that cannot be scaled right at the beginning itself.

Although the origin of life need not be a question which the evolutionist needs to answer, it is still a fundamental question that every evolutionist who is an atheist needs to answer. Who knows? Maybe, the origin of life research could discover new parameters which could make evolution by natural selection too simplistic. And if evolution does not need to explain the origin of life then what right does it have to claim that it has explained life?

Secondly, evolution did virtually nothing from the supposed beginning of life (nearly 3.8 billion years ago) up until 600 million years ago. Life was nothing more than single-celled bacteria and archaea for 3.2 billion years. Single-celled life diversified and adapted to various environments but remained single. Why did natural selection not bring about multicellularity at a time when all the major geological upheavals were happening? With no major complexity arising during this time, Mount Improbable has no slope to speak of here. Instead, it seems to be a plain road stretching for eighty percent of the journey to the top with a few minor bumps here and there.

The only major rise of complexity that happened during this time was the incredible jump from prokaryotes (cells without nucleus) to eukaryotes (with nucleus) around 1.5 billion years ago. Even this was not a gradual transition since we have no evidence of intermediaries. And the jump in complexity from prokaryotes to eukaryotes is so huge that Nick Lane calls it the "black hole at the heart of biology" in his book *The Vital Question*. Just peep through a microscope to compare a prokaryote to a eukaryote and see for yourself. The massive jump in complexity is simply astounding. The prokaryotes look like a home industry while the eukaryotes resemble giant factories that we see these days, with all their complicated and interconnected machinery. After the origin of life, this could easily be the second steepest slope on Mount Improbable that is impossible to scale.

It is important to note that there has been no major change in eukaryotes since they sprang into existence. They have remained the same for nearly 1.5 billion years. Every cell in a multicellular organism, be it a human or an octopus (including plants and trees) is made of the same eukaryote cell. Eukaryotes brought about all the staggering complexity and diversity without ever undergoing any change themselves. Which means that all mechanisms and processes needed to build complex life sprang out of nowhere when eukaryotes first appeared.

Thirdly, even if evolution claims to explain the origin of species, it has no clue how all the phyla originated, whose diversity is more fundamental and complex than species. In fact, the complexity and differentiation between various phyla makes speciation look like minor adaptations "after-its-kind." The Cambrian explosion brought about all the phyla and their fundamental body plans in a very short span of time. This is rapid prototyping at its best. It is important to note that there has been no development of new phyla since the Cambrian explosion. All the life we currently see on the planet, have their origins in the phyla that were formed suddenly 500 million years ago.

Not only did all the phyla, but their associated complexity like bilateral symmetry, multicellular complexity, sexual reproduction, and the process of morphogenesis together with the creation of specialized organs like the eyes were created in a blink of geological time during the Cambrian explosion. All these complexities are multiple steep slopes on Mount Improbable that cry out for an explanation. If this is not a decisive blow to gradual evolution, then what is?

Fourthly, fossil records clearly prove that gradual evolution is a myth. It has been known for a long time that life developed and diversified in sudden spurts followed by long periods of stasis—exactly opposite of what Darwin proposed. This observation has given rise to the "punctuated equilibrium" theory. There is no gradual evolution to speak of, and the sudden rise of complexity and diversity is a fact of the fossil record.

Lastly, we have clear empirical evidence that speciation can happen rapidly and does not need millions of years as proposed by Darwin. The species discovered in Lake Victoria invalidated two assumptions which evolutionists had made: That isolation was needed to create separate species and that it takes a long time of gradual evolution to form new species. The cichlid fish evolved so rapidly that it spawned 500 species in twelve thousand years flat, all in the same lake without any isolation. Such rapid speciation should bury the assumption of gradual evolution once for all. Dawkins cannot even go for a reprint of his misguided book when we have such clear empirical evidence of rapid development and diversification in nature.

If we closely scrutinize the mechanisms of evolution, we know of no other theory in science that begins with the most unscientific and irrational premise as this: Given time and chance, anything can happen. Its sole dependence on random chance makes it more faith-based than evidence-based. Take any other theory of science and it will roughly have the following deduction: A + B under conditions of C will always equal D. Moreover, this mathematical statement should have a correlation with what we observe in nature or can demonstrate in the lab. For example, two atoms of hydrogen plus one atom of oxygen under certain conditions equals to water. We can verify its constituents in the laboratory. Strangely, none of these sound principles of science apply to evolution. The origin of new species which are distinct and can no longer interbreed (especially those having different number of chromosomes) has neither been observed in nature nor demonstrated in the lab. The only vague equation that evolution can come up with is: A + random mutations (B) under fluke conditions (C) naturally selects D. How can this be a scientific theory when there is no certainty in what it is describing? In such a scenario, it can neither be falsified nor can it make accurate predictions.

No theory can be called scientific when it has randomness included in its core equations. In fact, appealing to randomness is antithetical to the scientific method. Science actively seeks order in nature and does not resign to random chaos. Evolution therefore cannot be a scientific theory because of its dependence on randomness and chance. There is no inevitability in its equations.

We currently know too little about life to commit to any theory. We have no clue if natural selection was enough or if there were other mechanisms at play. In such a scenario, we have to admit that there is no scientific theory of life—only an ill-informed, highly speculative, puerile commentary of life called evolution.

Atheists always overemphasize randomness in evolution, but how do they know that they are truly random? Because they cannot figure out any equations? How intellectually Ptolemaic is that? Random, chance, and fluke are mere English words which are devoid of meaning both in science and in a universe governed by the laws of physics. We already know of one entity, whose immediate workings may seem random, but clearly exhibits long-term order and purpose—a conscious intelligence. One may never be able to predict the next brush stroke of an artist who is painting a portrait, but when given enough time the painting takes on a perfectly cohesive shape in the end. One can never predict what steps each of us individually take to build a do-it-yourself toy airplane, but the toy airplane will be ready to glide once it is put together. In the subtlety of the laws of physics we see the humility of our Creator. Where the atheists see random chance, we see conscious design. As mentioned before, it is more rational to believe in the inevitability of intelligent causation than to believe in the improbability of random chance.

We already know in the context of fine-tuning (of the laws of physics) that there are nothing called "blind forces" in nature. Instead, it is the greatest oxymoron known to mankind that has been invented by the atheists. Guiding forces are exactly what you should expect to find in a universe that has a purpose. Once the initial conditions have been set, all the future states of the universe become inevitable—we were preplanned at the Big Bang.

We can therefore never know if mutations are really random, until we test that by simulating real randomness in the laboratory. Many experiments have already been done on this front but with negative results. They have been bombarding the genome of the fruit fly with x-rays for over a century now, yet they remain fruit flies—either grotesquely morphed or dead. All they have got are flies with legs in place of antennas, tinier eyes than usual or an additional set of useless wings.

If random changes can indeed bring about innovative code then why is there a software industry? Why do we need software developers? We can currently make millions of copies of a given code in a few minutes. Why doesn't the software industry introduce a few random changes while making millions of copies to get an updated version of their software? They can easily simulate natural selection by testing the software on the fly for new features that needs to be there in the new version. If we are unable to do this for simple software code, how do the evolutionists expect the same to happen in nature for the complex genetic code? From a programming perspective, evolution by random mutations is the bigger delusion.

We already know of a phenomenon that appears random in the short term but where order emerges in the long term: radioactivity. We have no clue when each individual particle will decay, but we can exactly predict its half-life. We have no clue how such order emerges from chaos, but it does. Half-life is deterministic but individual decay is not. Even all the molecular activities that happen at a frenetic pace inside a living cell seem random and chaotic but nothing is further from the truth. This should teach us not to call something random just because we cannot compute an equation to comprehend it. It is against the very spirit of science that is striving to find order in the universe.

Evolutionists believe that most mutations are harmful and the beneficial ones are very rare. They postulate that there is a one in a million chance that it will be favourable. Most mutations they say are either useless, detrimental, or fatal. If most of the mutations are harmful then why has evolution not favoured accurate replicators thereby freezing evolution altogether? "Impossible," asserts P. Z. Myers, associate professor of biology at the University of Minnesota without specifying any concrete scientific reasons and conveniently choosing to ignore the existence of what are called "living fossils." These are species that have not changed for millions of years, like the horseshoe crab and the ginkgo tree.

The ground reality is something else. No book on evolution tells you this but there is already an error-checking mechanism in place in every cell.   As James A. Shapiro describes in his book *Evolution: A view from the 21ˢᵗ Century* that DNA proofreading and repair systems are central to the yin and yang of cell management of genome structures. In fact, the Nobel Prize for chemistry in 2015 was awarded to Tomas Lindahl, Paul Modrich, and Aziz Sancar for discovering how DNA repairs itself.

What no book on evolution tells you is the amazing self-organization that is found in life. When the chromosome of Deinococcus radiodurans is subjected to intense ionizing radiation of more than 500,000 rads and blown to smithereens within the cell, the chromosome will automatically reassemble itself in 12 to 24 hours flat, ready to take on the world again.

What no book on evolution tells you is the remarkable protein found in tardigrades that protects its genome from potential damage due to harmful radiation (New Scientist: "World's hardiest animal has evolved radiation shield for its DNA," dated 20 September 2016.) Called "damage suppressor," it forms a protective cocoon around the DNA without disrupting its normal functions. Nature has already moved in the direction of eliminating mutations. Why such self-preserving and self-repairing replicators did not get naturally selected and eliminate evolution altogether is a question that every evolutionist needs to answer.

Even if the cosmological fine-tuning does not convince these eternal pessimists then surely the fine-tuning of protein folding should convince the hardest of sceptics. This is a process that happens every second in the cell of every living being on the planet. A polypeptide chain after it has been generated out of the ribosome has an astronomical number of ways it can freely fold. One estimate of possibilities made by Cyrus Levinthal is 10^{143} (one followed by one hundred and forty-three zeroes—to have a better perspective, there are only 10^{80} particles in the entire universe.) That is how many different ways a protein can potentially fold. Yet among them only one particular type of folding is useful and all the others are useless, some could be harmful for the organism. If the protein tried all of those configurations before "naturally selecting" the right one, it would have taken longer than the time our universe has existed. Reason why it is called "Levinthal's paradox." But remarkably, the protein folds up accurately to the useful configuration even as it is coming out of the ribosome. Although scientists have made many speculations, we still have no clue of how that happens. One thing needs to be clarified here: even if this "protein folding" problem can someday be explained by physics and chemistry, it still is a decisive blow to evolution by natural selection. If there is anyone out there still talking about a blind watchmaker, he is blind while he sees.

It is this self-organizing complexity among other things that has led a number of scientists to doubt that random mutations and natural selection alone are sufficient to explain the complexity found in life. There are currently two camps within the evolutionists. The reductionist ones—naturally, all militant atheists belong to this camp, and the anti-reductionists like Stuart Kauffman and Stephen J. Gould, who believe that we are missing something really big in the equation of life. Stuart Kauffman in his book *The Origins of Order* argues that natural selection is not enough to explain the overwhelming and beautiful order found in nature. James A. Shapiro in his book *Evolution: A View from the 21st Century* clearly articulates that it is innovation, and not natural selection, that is the critical issue in evolution. To conveniently assume innovation for natural selection to sift through is unwarranted.

Natural selection is therefore a convenient cop out that every atheist resorts to. It may be alright to use certain assumptions in a hypothesis, but when those assumptions turn into assertions, it ceases to be science and becomes a dogma.

Whether the evolutionists believe in irreducibly complex systems or not, there is one such scenario that is impossible to avoid. I call it the "device driver" problem and this is irreducible at the fundamental level. Suppose you plug in a device (like a mouse) to your laptop. The operating system searches for a preinstalled device driver, loads it, and prepares it for use. But how do living systems do that? For living organisms, it is the brain that processes information. It uses the input from our sensors like eye, nose, or ears and sends the output to the central nervous system to act upon them. We now know that the genes that make my brain—my processor—will be situated in a different place than the ones that make my eye—my input system. It is also different from the genes that make my legs—my output system. The problem is that unless all evolve together in a coordinated way, they will remain useless on their own and there will be no "natural selection" to speak of. If the sensors of my eye mutate to see x-rays but the brain is not ready to process them, it will treat those signals as garbage. Until the brain also mutates to process the x-rays, the new signals from the eye will have no selective advantage. And to complete the circuit, if the brain does not correctly interpret the signal and tell my legs to scram, the new features of my eye and my brain have no selective advantage. Needless to say, there have to be mutations in all three places simultaneously—in the input system, in the processing system, and in the output system—to have a selective advantage. If there is anyone out there, even from a reputed university like Oxford, telling me that all of them could have happened simultaneously by fluke, then we have only two things to say to such a deluded lot: firstly, that is an unscientific assertion which we reject with a firm conviction, and secondly, they are in urgent need of a psychiatrist!

The cell itself is irreducibly complex. The DNA cannot express itself without the environment of the cell and vice versa. If we remove the DNA, the cell dies and if we extract and isolate the DNA, it cannot generate the rest of the cell by itself. Both need each other and cannot do without the other. The genetic code on its own is as useless as a compact disk without a CD player. What more evidence do they need for irreducibly complex systems? This is as clear and in your face as it gets.

The evolutionists continually brainwash us to believe that the survival of the fittest is the norm in nature but deeper analysis of nature shows exactly the opposite. The eukaryotic cell may have been the result of different micro-organisms merging together in a symbiotic relationship. The human body is also a biosphere of collaboration between all sorts of bacteria that help us get along in life. It should be a surprise to the evolutionists that we have not been decimated by those very microbes that reside in us, considering their quicker reproductive and mutation rates compared to ours. Coming to our planet itself, we now know that it has a delicately balanced ecosystem where no single organism can afford to dominate without upsetting its ecological balance.

If evolution is indeed a continuous process then why do we not see continuous evolution of prokaryotes into eukaryotes, the various stages of multicellular evolution, or the development of new organs? Since the prokaryotes have been around continuously for billions of years, we should be seeing the snapshots of all the different stages of evolution that has happened in the past reenacted before our eyes at any given point of time. How come we do not see those in nature? We should at the least be seeing multiple transitions between prokaryotes to eukaryotes, but the brute fact is that we don't.

If there is a scientific theory that is top heavy with unproven speculations then evolution would be awarded the Nobel Prize by an overwhelming margin. And most of those speculations are superficial "just-so" stories that they imagine without presenting hard evidence. Only when we really delve into what evolution has actually explained can we clearly see that this emperor has no clothes. It definitely does not explain any of the fundamental questions regarding living systems. It has no clue about the origin of life or the creation of life that happens millions of times every day—morphogenesis. It has no clue how the major transitions like prokaryotes to eukaryotes, unicellular to multicellular, or asexual to sexual reproduction could have occurred. It has no clue how all the phyla came about in a blink of geological time and never since. It has no clue how consciousness arose, leave alone why it exists.

Instead, evolution conveniently assumes the complex machinery of life found in a cell while having no clue how it originated. We have no clue how the genetic code originated and what ninety-five percent of the genome does. What we know is the five percent that codes for proteins which are like Lego blocks. Beyond that, we have no clue how the morphology itself emerges. They naively assert that morphogenesis is simple origami even while having no clue how complex organisms develop as per the genetic code.

All that we have learned in school about evolution and what Darwin said is turning out to be false in the light of current research. Darwin thought life could have emerged from a warm little pond, he was dead wrong. They initially thought that a living cell was a featureless blob of protoplasm, they were dead wrong. Darwin thought life developed gradually in millions of years (now billions). He was wrong in context of the Cambrian explosion and the punctuated equilibrium theory. He envisaged a grand tree of life but was wrong—current research in genetics has already buried the tree of life (New Scientist: "Darwin was wrong: cutting down the tree of life" dated 24 January 2009.) In fact, American biotechnologist Craig Venter finds it meaningless to map life in any reasonable way because the lateral gene transfers observed in nature have complicated things further. If one were to pick different genes from within the same genome, they will generate a different tree of life.

Scientists predicted that Homo sapiens would have at least hundred thousand genes, they were dead wrong. We have as few as a worm, just around twenty-three thousand. They thought genes alone are enough, but once again they have been proved wrong. Genetic code is not the whole story, epigenetics is an emerging field of research. Haeckel's images of early embryos were outright fraud, yet that is exactly what one should expect to see if evolution were true—a recapitulation of the recent forms during morphogenesis—but we simply don't.

Two recent findings should be deeply disturbing to every evolutionist. New research done in Rockefeller University on the early embryonic development of humans undermines evolution in a very radical way. Mice and human genes are ninety-seven percent identical and therefore it is natural to assume that our embryonic development will be similar to a great extent. But by studying the human blastocyte and comparing it with that of a mouse, researchers found surprising results. It was earlier believed that that these pathways are evolutionarily conserved and similar. But this has been empirically observed to be plain wrong. With respect to the time of onset of differentiation and the pathways taken, humans fundamentally differ from mice. Cell lineage is species specific. What sense does it make then to say humans evolved from mice like mammals or apes when their developmental pathways are so fundamentally different?

The second finding is the recent analysis of the COI (cytochrome oxidase I) barcodes of various species done by Mark Stoeckel and David Thaler at the same Rockefeller University in New York which showed that ninety percent of the species currently living on our planet originated a mere 100 to 200 thousand years ago!

Why then is Darwin still venerated despite getting so many things wrong? The atheist will say that their bible *On the Origin of Species* may have many flaws, but it is the central idea that is important. Why then can we not use the same logic regarding the Holy Bible and the central idea that there is a theistic Creator God? Why get petty regarding the details? And why such double standards? Even if one does not agree with everything that is written in the Holy Bible, it should not stop one from believing in the central idea that there is a Creator God, that Jesus Christ is a historical figure, and that He is the chief corner stone of our ethical framework.

Evolution needs a reality check and we can already hear the distant thunder in fields of molecular biology, microbiology, developmental biology, and genetics. I think we are poised for a major paradigm shift as new findings confound the theory of evolution in a fundamental way and from the complexity found inside the black box of Darwin—the living cell. In the light of current research, we should perhaps rephrase Theodosius Dobzhansky: "Nothing in evolution is making sense anymore in the light of microbiology and genetics."

If there is any place in science that we have to reiterate the motto of the Royal Society: *nullius in verba* (which roughly means "take nobody's word for it") then it is in the biology classes where evolution is taught as dogmatic ideology. And if there was ever a place to promote a questioning mind, it is among students of the biological sciences.

Indeed, there are many aspects of evolution that are questioned every day. That evolution is essentially a random process has been falsified after it was discovered that related species evolve similar physical traits independently using the same genes. Convergence is a fact of life observable in nature (New Scientist: "Evolution returns to the same old genes again and again," dated 23 August 2003.) We also know that rewinding the tape of life will not be always random as it should be if it is dependent of random mutations. But it will always bring about intelligent human beings like us (New Scientist: "Tape of life may not always be random," dated 26 January 2015.) The myth that life needs long periods of time to bring about new species has already been falsified in nature (New Scientist: "Why evolution is going nowhere fast," dated 30 March 2011.)

New evidence is emerging which may force us to rethink both the "selfish gene" and the Darwin's version of evolutionary theory. We have begun to see experimental evidence that individuals can acquire characteristics through interaction with their environment and then pass these on to their offspring (New Scientist: "Rewriting Darwin: The new non-genetic inheritance," dated 9 July 2008.) Botanists have long known such "transgenerational epigenetic inheritance," but now a flood of evidence is convincing the zoologists as well.

If individual genes are the units of selection (as proposed by Richard Dawkins in his book *The Selfish Gene*) and gradual evolution is true, then one should expect to see more DNA in humans than in single-celled organisms. We don't—certain amoebae have much more DNA than humans. We should expect more genes in humans than in fish. We don't—we have as few genes as a puny worm (approximately twenty-three thousand.) Does the number of chromosomes give any indication? It doesn't—potatoes have more chromosomes (48) than humans (46.) We should expect all the genes in the genome to be functional since they are units under selection pressure. We don't, and we have no clue what more than 80 percent of the genome does. If they are trying to tell us that they do not have defined functions, then that is evidence of "unnatural" selection which neither the selfish gene theory, nor evolution predicts. Imagine an organism with 80 percent of its organs being just freeloaders without specific function.

The genome is turning out to be more complicated than we thought. Does the genome always parse its code in the same way? It doesn't. Grasshoppers and locusts have the same genome, yet differ remarkably in their morphology. The queen bee and the worker bees have the same genome, but differ in their form and function according to the diet fed to them. Genes are also context sensitive. If you take the "eye genes" of a mouse and inject it into a fly's genome, you will get eyes of a fly instead of the eyes of a mouse. It has also been observed in a few cases that the genes continue to function normally in spite of radical mutations (pdx1 gene in a sand rat is an example.) The latest news in genetics is the discovery of dark DNA (or the realization that some genes are missing in the chromosomes.) It has been discovered that a few species of rats and birds seem to have features that are not encoded in the chromosome, yet have RNA transcripts in the nucleus that generate those features. All such intriguing experimental results clearly show that we have a long way to go before we understand the complexity of morphogenesis and life. We don't know what implications these experiments have for the theory of evolution. We should therefore stop claiming that man descended from apes until we resolve these conundrums.

The good news is that the theory of evolution is itself evolving (New Scientist: "Evolution evolves: Beyond the selfish gene," dated 24 September 2016.) In the beginning, the reductionists said it was design without intelligence and now they are saying it is intelligence without design (New Scientist: "Intelligence without design," dated 22 March 2016.) Whatever new form the theory of evolution takes, it is beginning to look more and more complex than it was naively assumed during Darwin's time. Even if the sceptics are not convinced yet, we believe future research will clearly and unambiguously vindicate intelligent causation.

With so many concepts of this outdated theory of the Victorian age proven to be wrong we should quit calling it the theory of evolution any longer. It has been proposed that we rename it "Postmodern Hypothesis" or "An Extended Evolutionary Synthesis," (New Scientist: "Evolution evolves: Beyond the selfish gene," dated 24 September 2016.) But I would rather rename it as the Teleological Development of Life. We should stop talking about the "evolution" of life and instead speak about the "development" of life to distinguish between the old and the new paradigms.

Before the atheistic cowboys jump the gun, we need to clarify what teleology means and how we can scientifically test this concept. How does one make out if an action is intentionally purposed or not? With conscious beings, it is out of scope for scientists. They will never know if I intended to do something or not, because they simply don't understand the human brain to that extent yet. Suppose I claim that I did not intend to kill the deluded zoologist in Oxford and that he just got in the way on a trekking path where I was testing my remote-controlled gun! If I feigned my innocence well, there would be no way of knowing that I intended to kill him. But suppose they find a note book in my house which lays down the plan with steps in detail, there is no question that the murder was intended and therefore teleological.

Ditto for life. Teleology is right before us in the form of the genetic code and we have failed to see it. In the euphoria of discovery, we have forgotten the inventor. Life is a product of purposeful design directed by the genetic code. There is no blind chance here.

Suppose I land on a distant planet and discover a hard disc which has detailed instructions on how to survive on the planet that I have landed on. It is clear that whoever has put the instructions there intended that I should survive on that planet. Those instructions are teleological in every sense. I always wondered why the blokes who discovered the genetic code went to the pub to announce it, instead of going straight to church and demanding the choir to sing "How great thou art" hymn!

We can extend teleology to the universe itself. As mentioned before, the laws and constants of nature that guide the development of our universe are exactly what one would expect to see if it had a set goal or purpose. But in a purposeless universe, we should be seeing a random and chaotic universe which has no stable laws of physics or chemistry to direct its development. That there are forces to guide the universe in a definitive way is clear evidence of teleology. With the discovery of fine-tuning of these laws and constants, there is no doubt that the universe was expecting us. No amount of rhetoric from the atheistic camp is going to convince us otherwise.

Atheists usually resort to their "trivialize and dismiss" strategy to counter such evidence of intelligence and teleology. They point to a few "flaws" in design and mock intelligent causation. We have already shown how such arguments fail to convince. If I make a robot whose processor can detect its own deficiencies and correct them then I would be called an extraordinary genius. It is really funny to see a side-note in a book describing our wondrous brain that says it is not intelligently designed because of the extra length of the recurrent laryngeal nerve of a giraffe (The Brain—Beginners Guides.) I think we know where this flapdoodle is coming from, especially since it is a publication based out of Oxford. As pointed out earlier, it is like someone walking into a complex data centre and getting astounded by the complexity of multiple servers interconnected with intricate wiring, switches, and routers. And on his way out conclude that it was not intelligently designed because he saw some extra bit of a cable somewhere. How incredibly biased can one get?

Such examples are abundant in atheistic literature. When they see a less optimized design, they mock God, but when they see astounding intricate design, they claim that to be a "miracle of evolution." Thereby invoking the second greatest oxymoron that mankind has ever heard. If they profess to be unbiased, they should do the opposite and humbly admit that the brain has overwhelming evidence of intelligent causation with a few minor exceptions. Statistically speaking, design wins hands down and no rational mind will side these minor exceptions. All the supposed "flaws" pales in comparison to the brilliance of the self-organizing complexity found in nature and the fine-tuning of the universe itself. It is therefore more rational to believe that the less optimized entities were the result of low priority than to believe the highly optimized ones came by sheer dumb luck.

There are others who ask whimsical "why" questions to express their scepticism. As pointed out earlier, these cannot be scientific or rational questions, but always tend to be whimsical. For example, they ask why God took so long to create us. They conveniently forget that all of space-time, matter, and the laws of physics that are needed to make us was created in a fraction of a second, in a twinkling of an eye at the Big Bang. And without enzymes—the catalysts of life—it would have taken trillions of years more to create complex life. Besides, we are not sure what their grouse is, it is not like they were waiting in the lobby for that long until their parents met! We have already seen that there is no absolute time according to the theory of relativity. "But, beloved, be not ignorant of this one thing, that one day is with the Lord as a thousand years, and a thousand years as one day." (2 Peter 3:8.)

As mentioned earlier, we have no pretensions of knowing the answer to every "why" question they come up with, but at the same time we think they are pointless. No amount of reasoning from our side will be accepted by the atheists and no answer to those questions will ever have the potential to shake the other powerful evidence that we find for the existence of God in nature.

Many atheists typically point to the violence found in nature and ask how a benevolent Creator could have allowed it. Once again, we should remember that these are not scientific questions but theological ones. And biblically speaking, that is exactly what we should be observing in nature according to the Christian worldview—a brilliant creation gone awry because of the fall of man, and a creation banished from the Creator's presence. In contrast, one just needs to read the prophecy of Isaiah to know how a world will be in the future when we reconcile with our Creator: "The wolf also shall dwell with the lamb, and the leopard shall lie down with the kid; and the calf and the young lion and the fatling together; and a little child shall lead them…They shall not hurt nor destroy in all my holy mountain: for the earth shall be full of the knowledge of the Lord, as the waters cover the sea." (Isaiah 11:6-9.)

The problem with the atheists is that they do theology when they ought to be doing biology, for example: Darwin pointing to the Ichneumon larva and how it feeds on the insides of the caterpillars, and do biology when they ought to be doing theology, for example: the creation narrative of the Holy Bible. They also somehow assume that they get a free doctorate in theology when they graduate in physics, chemistry, or biology. But the ground reality is something else. Richard Feynman was spot on when he confessed the following: "I believe that a scientist looking at nonscientific problems is just as dumb as the next guy."

Before we end this chapter, it is important to note that even if the atheists insist that some form of evolution is true, it still does not make atheism true. At the most it could force one to be a deist instead of theist. Fossils of extinct animals does not invalidate intelligent causation in the same way that the presence of vintage cars and airplanes do not invalidate the existence of intelligent engineers. In a way, it actually validates intelligent foresight because it means that life has been made incredibly elastic from the ground up to adapt to every nook and corner of our planet soon after the fundamental body plans were put in place during the Cambrian period. Francis Collins who spearheaded the National Human Genome Research Institute, founded and served as president of The BioLogos Foundation, which promotes discourse on the relationship between science and religion and advocates the perspective that belief in Christianity can be reconciled with acceptance of evolution and science. In 2009, Pope Benedict XVI appointed Collins to the Pontifical Academy of Sciences. Collins has also written a number of books on science, medicine, and religion including the New York Times bestseller: *The Language of God: A Scientist Presents Evidence for Belief.*

Key Summary

When we examine what evolution has really explained, we realize that this emperor has no clothes. It has no clue how life originated, how the atoms of life (prokaryotes and eukaryotes) originated, how the fundamental body plans of all living organisms originated, how all the major transitions of life came to be, and lastly how life is created everyday via morphogenesis. Evolution is therefore much ado about nothing.

No theory can be called scientific when it has randomness included in its core equations. In fact, appealing to randomness is antithetical to the scientific method. Science actively seeks order in nature and does not resign to random chaos. Evolution therefore cannot be a scientific theory because of its dependence on randomness and chance. There is no inevitability in its equations.

Many aspects of evolution have turned out to be false. We currently know too little about life to commit to any theory. We have no clue if natural selection was enough or if there were other mechanisms at play. In such a scenario, we have to admit that there is no scientific theory of life—only an ill-informed, highly speculative, puerile commentary of life called evolution.

Overwhelming evidence for God

Before we present evidence for the existence of God, we would like to know what kind of evidence do the atheists want? And what kind of evidence will convince them? Lawrence Krauss says that if the stars lined up to form the words "I exist," then they would believe that God exists. But will they really? If they are attributing the astonishing fine-tuning found in the universe to chance and fluke, what is the guarantee that they will not dismiss the star formation as fluke too?

Isn't that a naive expectation even after seeing such overwhelming evidence from astronomy and biology? Is not the power, order, and wisdom found in nature saying that He exists? Is not the fine-tuning of the laws of physics and the constants of nature saying that He exists? Is not the complexity found in the living cell screaming the words "I exist?"

Ironically, in current debates it is the theists who have begun to present empirical evidence for the existence of God and it is the atheists who are resorting to unproven speculative myths, philosophy, whim, and blind faith. In science, empirical evidence has much more value than a speculative hypothesis because an ugly empirical fact can demolish a beautiful theory. Einstein rightly pointed out that no amount of experimentation can prove a theory right, but one single experiment can prove it false. Facts that can be empirically verified are more important than ideas (speculations) that have no evidence. A few examples given below should make it clear.

When we point to the first cause or the eternal source that brought about all the energy, laws, and fine-tuning, they speculate that those could have come out of nothing and without any cause—which by the way, is the very definition of a miracle. It is both unscientific and irrational to claim that it is "natural" for a universe to pop out of absolutely nothing. The first cause or the eternal source is itself overwhelming evidence for the existence of a Creator. Whatever science chooses to call this entity, we revere that entity as our Creator God. We owe our very existence to this entity and this conclusion is as rational and scientific as it can get.

When we specifically point to the fine-tuning of our universe, they resort to unproven speculative myths like the inflationary universe, parallel universes, or the landscape of string theory. None of them have the general consensus that "the standard model" of physics has in the scientific community today. Parallel universes and string theories are neither empirically verifiable, demonstrable, nor observable. All such theories are invisible fire-breathing dragons in Carl Sagan's garage.

They setup huge radio telescopes to detect intelligent signals coming from outer space in their search for extra-terrestrials. But when they do find solid empirical evidence of intelligence in the fine-tuning of the laws of physics they become Holocaust deniers. The first cause and the initial conditions are incredibly more powerful evidence of intelligent causation than a puerile radio signal from outer space.

When we point to the complexity involved in the origin of life (even Nobel Prize winners died scratching their heads over this one) they choose to place blind faith on the unproven hypothesis of abiogenesis. Even when it has been continually falsified for over a century since it was first hypothesized. They assume blind chance could account for the origin of life even while having no clue what it takes to create life in the first place. Faith couldn't be more blinder than this. It is time for the biologists to stop being modern-day alchemists and admit that there is no chemical pathway to creating an info processing system called life.

We now know that the living cell is much more than physics and chemistry—it is an information processing system. Currently, the only known entity that can invent information processing systems is a conscious intelligence. This is clear evidence of top-down design. Yet they continue to have blind faith that a storm in a junkyard assembled a jumbo jet by chance. Such bias is unparalleled in the sciences. It is more rational to believe in the inevitability of conscious design (whose examples we can see in everyday technology) than to believe in the improbability of random chance. The Noble Laureate Christian de Duve has indeed argued for a "rejection of improbabilities so incommensurably high that they can only be called miracles, phenomena that fall outside the scope of scientific enquiry."

When we point to morphogenesis, the most complex process in the known universe, which has clear and unambiguous evidence of intelligence (the greatest code breaker of Great Britain died scratching his head over this one), they continue to delude themselves thinking it gradually evolved over billions of years. The brute fact is that it happened very rapidly during the Cambrian explosion. In fact, Lewis Wolpert, the developmental biologist, thinks that very few new development rules have appeared since the Cambrian. We find the same homeobox genes used in species that shared a common ancestor six hundred million years ago—around the time of the Cambrian explosion.

From a purely coding perspective, morphogenesis cannot be a bottom-up design since the code found in every cell of our body is the same. Yet there are more than 200 different types of cells in the body. It is like the same code churning out different micro-organisms. Although we know that the epigenetic markers create the differentiation, we should remember that they also add a new layer of complexity. What guides the epigenetic markers to precisely switch on at the right time and place? Besides, as far as we know the genes code only for proteins—the Lego blocks of life—but we still have no clue how different shapes arise from these Lego blocks. Whatever the answer, such clockwork mechanisms are clear evidence of top-down design. "…for I am fearfully and wonderfully made:" (Psalms 139:14.)

When we point to the major transitions of life and their associated complexity, they have blind faith that natural selection is enough to explain such complexity, even while having no clue what it takes to bring about those major transitions in the first place. When we point to the sudden appearance of all the fundamental body plans (phyla) of animals found today in the Cambrian explosion that makes speciation look like petty adaptations, they eternally hope that it will be explained away someday. The Cambrian evidence is so strong that in the nineteenth century, many thought that life itself began only during the Cambrian period. Even Darwin himself admitted that the Cambrian explosion was an inexplicable mystery to him.

When we present the evidence of complexity found in our brain, they blithely believe that the device and its software (device driver) can appear magically by sheer dumb luck at exactly the same time. They conveniently forget that it needs top-down design to create complex information processing systems. We now have clear empirical evidence that we are indeed very special in the universe because we possess the most complex entity in the entire known universe! We may not be the physical center of the universe, but we certainly are the intellectual center of the universe. We are the only ones who have rationally deduced that our Creator must necessarily exist and are aware of His wonderous creation!

When we present the phenomena of consciousness, they dismiss it as a pointless epiphenomenon even while having no clue what it takes for an entity to become conscious in the first place. When we point to the first-person perception of free will, they say even that it is an illusion, thereby rendering our scientific and rational endeavours pointless.

Even emergent phenomena are evidence of intelligent causation. We see many such examples in nature wherein the whole is much more than the sum of its parts. You could use every part of a car for other purposes, but only when it is assembled fully will it have the emergent property of transportation. The atheists can delude themselves that those emerging properties came about by fluke but we interpret all emergent phenomena as clear evidence of teleology, of methodical planning and foresight. Consider the simple example of water which is crucial for life. Two atoms of Hydrogen and one atom of Oxygen makes a molecule of water, but the emerging properties of water cannot be deduced by analyzing the individual atoms of hydrogen and oxygen. Water is incredibly weird in many ways; it has nearly 72 anomalies and its physical and chemical properties are very different from any other liquids we know (New Scientist: "Tapping the incredible weirdness of water," dated 4 April 2015.)

Near-death experiences are another body of evidence which is becoming increasingly difficult to ignore. Doctors and physicians around the world have known about these experiences from their patients (including small children) for a long time, but they have either ignored them or have been unduly dismissive. Fortunately for science, many doctors like Dr. Eben Alexander have themselves had these experiences and have written about them. It is important to note that most of these experiences are remarkably consistent—they all see an approaching light, they all see a review of their past life, they all see relatives who had died before them, and most of them have out-of-body experiences that are so vivid that it takes an incredible bias to dismiss them. In fact, few of them describe what was happening around them in graphic detail even when their ECG was showing a flatline (which means they were clinically dead.) These records are not only evidence for afterlife, but also for the Christian worldview since most eastern religions believe in rebirth which these NDEs clearly refute. A detailed research has been done on this by many doctors and physicians like Dr. Raymond Moody, Dr. Sam Parnia, and Dr. Jeffery Long. They have presented their research in books which are out there for anyone wanting to examine the evidence. *Evidence of the Afterlife: The Science of Near-Death Experiences* by Jeffery Long & Paul Perry and *Life after Death: The Evidence* by Dinesh D'souza are two books which are recommended reading on this subject.

Predictably, the atheists are invariably dismissive of the research done on NDEs, and the evidence that is presented. For us, it is more rational to believe the physicians on the ground who have gathered plenty of indisputable evidence rather than the just-so speculations that come out of the ivory towers of materialism. Those who have experienced NDEs may well turn out to be the involuntary Magellan's and Columbus' of new dimensions of reality.

Emergent properties therefore cannot be called "natural" in any sense because they are neither predictable nor rationally deducible. Emergence and irreducibly complex systems are two sides of the same coin. Both of them together raise many questions which Darwinian evolution cannot answer.

All the evidence presented in this chapter are empirical—we can currently observe and detect them in nature. While most atheistic answers are either irrational (that machines can think,) unscientific (like abiogenesis,) or based on unproven speculations (like landscape of string theory or parallel universes.) The atheists can delude themselves into thinking that the universe came out of nothing, or that life arose accidently in a warm little pond, and the complexity found in life is the result of random mutations, but they cannot call it science. All these are atheistic assertions made out of blind faith.

If extraordinary claims need extraordinary evidence then the first cause, the fine-tuning of the laws and constants of physics, the complexity of living cells, and morphogenesis—the most complex process in the universe, which goes on to make the most complex entity in the universe called the human brain—are the extraordinary evidence that we present for a powerful and intelligent Creator. It cannot get any more extraordinary than this. And all the evidence given above are empirical.

That science will one day answer all the above questions is irrelevant to the point of discussion and the validity of the evidence presented here. We are pointing to what we know to be incredibly complex and not to some mystery which science may answer one day. As pointed out earlier, knowing how an automobile engine works does not mean that Ford does not exist. Whether God brought about the complexity by intervening (theistic view) or by automating (deistic view) is beside the point. The fact of the matter is that it takes incredible power, order, and wisdom to make a universe that is capable of life. If they are telling me that nature is smart enough to bring about all the above then that is pantheism—a belief that our Creator and nature are one and the same.

Scientific methodology does not allow one to be a soothsayer or a prophet. If they are speculating that the atheistic worldview will be vindicated some day in the future, then it could equally devastate their worldview one day. Who knows, maybe science will discover a hidden organizing principle that explains both the formation of a living cell and complex multi-cellular organisms (via morphogenesis) thereby drastically altering our perspective and falsifying evolution by random mutations.

If extraordinary claims need extraordinary evidences then it should work both ways. We find it extraordinarily naive that the universe could have come about from absolutely nothing and that a storm in a junkyard could bring about a jumbo jet (abiogenesis.) Or that a physical system like a computer can develop consciousness when it reaches a certain complexity. Or that morphogenesis is nothing but simple origami. All these assertions are extraordinary claims made by atheists, for which they have zilch evidence. They can go on speculating until kingdom come, but until those speculations are verified by experimental evidence they have no right to call it science. As far as we know, these are modern-day speculative myths and assertions coming from a biased reductionist mind.

We dare say that if Darwin was around to see the astonishing inner complexity of a living cell which electron microscopes have revealed to us and the fine-tuning of the universe, he would have no doubts about the existence of God. Although he may have died an atheist, he was already beginning to have doubts when he scribbled the following in his diary: "The extreme difficulty or rather impossibility of conceiving this immense and wonderful universe, including man with his capability of looking far backwards and far into the futurity, as a result of blind chance or necessity. When thus reflecting I feel compelled to look to a first cause having an intelligent mind in some degree analogous to that of man; and I deserve to be called a Theist." Unfortunately, his pet dogs aren't getting the drift yet.

Many atheists become unduly sceptical when we present empirical facts and claim that even if the evidence proves intelligence, it does not necessarily mean that He is the God of Abraham. This is plain sophistry. Any entity who can create the universe out of nothing and has the wisdom to create life and consciousness, then that entity by definition is our Creator God. What name He has is irrelevant to the debate. It is silly of the atheists to make this a debate on nomenclature and semantics.

If they want more evidence than what is presented here or if they want to know more about this Creator God, then that can happen only through revelation. Since the phenomenon decides how it will be detected, God decides how He will be detected. "...holiness, without which no man shall see the Lord." (Hebrews 12:14.) Knowledge and detectors become secondary and character becomes primary. The humble have gone that way and have known Him, while the proud laze around in their veranda and demand God to come and shake their hands. No wonder the Bible speaks about a time when God will make foolish the wisdom of this world (I Corinthians 1:20.)

We have to admit that we do not have the ability to go back in time with a digicam and record the act of creation by God. Or even getting a live recording of the Sermon on the Mount. But just to set the record straight, we are not the ones who are looking for more evidence. If they want more evidence then they can go back in time and shake the hands of Jesus or go even further back in time and shake hands with the Creator Himself. This is not some funny and humorous proposition, but a powerful reminder of the limits of science and knowledge in the dimension of space and time.

The onus now shifts to the atheists. They have to explain how our universe popped out of nothing, how life popped out of a chemical broth, how consciousness arises in the brain, and explain countless other problems of evolution like the major transitions and the Cambrian explosion. Dogmatic assertions, speculations, rhetoric, smart talk, and bestselling paperbacks are inadmissible in the court of law.

There are many scientists who do not ponder on these deeper issues and go on in their life doing specialized research which they are paid to do. They are the boring lot, whose god is their belly. There are many others who acknowledge that God exists, but are too busy or lazy to research and subscribe to any specific religion. Some carelessly subscribe to the one they are born into. Few others are skeptical of all religions even though they agree that God exists. It is important to remember that no religion may have a complete revelation of God since He is infinite in every aspect, but a good working model will do. In science, we don't have a grand unified theory but the "Standard Model" is a good working model everyone accepts. In the same way, Christianity is the "Standard Model" that we recommend for humanity.

Key Summary

In current debates on God's existence, it is the theists who have begun to present empirical evidence for the existence of God and it is the atheists who are resorting to unproven speculative myths, philosophy, whim, and blind faith. In science, empirical evidence has much more value than a speculative hypothesis because an ugly fact can demolish a beautiful theory. Einstein rightly pointed out that no amount of experimentation can prove a theory right, but one single experiment can prove it false. Facts that can be empirically verified are more important than ideas (speculations) that have no evidence.

If extraordinary claims need extraordinary evidence then the first cause, the fine-tuning of the laws and constants of physics, the complexity of living cells, and morphogenesis—the most complex process in the universe, which goes on to make the most complex entity in the universe called the human brain—are the extraordinary evidences that we present for a powerful and intelligent Creator. It cannot get any more extraordinary than this.

If extraordinary claims need extraordinary evidences then it should work both ways. We find it extraordinarily naive that the universe could have come about from absolutely nothing and that a storm in a junkyard could bring about a jumbo jet (abiogenesis.) Or that a physical system like a computer can develop consciousness when it reaches a certain complexity. Or that morphogenesis is nothing but simple origami. As far as we know, these are modern-day speculative myths and assertions coming from a biased reductionist mind.

What has atheism got to do with humanism?

Every religion is characterized not only by a belief in God but also by its moral code. Jews have their Torah, the Buddhists have their Dhammapada, and the Christians have the Gospels. But where do atheists get their moral code from? If we delve a little deeper and search for the basis of their morality, it will become abundantly clear that even this emperor has no clothes.

Anthony Grayling, the British philosopher, claims that there are no a-theists just as there are no a-stamp collectors (those who do not collect stamps as a hobby) and they have nothing to say about God and religion until they have sufficient evidence to convince them. If we go by this logic then they are a-moral as well, because there cannot be any code of conduct attached to a-stamp collectors.

It is a mistake to assume like many do, that atheism is equal to secular humanism. It is not. There is no connecting dot between them. Their worldview is devoid of any moral imperatives and will inevitably end up in nihilism or cynicism. Reason why some could even turn out to be Maoists or Communists. What about pyromaniacs claiming their right to gene expression? Who is to stop them and on what basis?

Historically, atheists were moral relativists—those who believe that morals are cultural and parochial. In this, they were at least honest in evaluating the consequences of their worldview which was based on scientific materialism and evolution. But somewhere down the line a random mutation seems to have changed them into moral realists—the belief that there are moral absolutes independent of culture. Unfortunately, the new atheists are not even honest in evaluating the consequences of their worldview. The only basis for moral realism can be theism.

Atheism based on scientific materialism will incline more towards nihilism, skepticism, and cynicism because according to them, we are "nothing but" chemical scum on a speck of dust in this vast cosmos. Their belief that there is no meaning or purpose in life is clearly nihilistic. Since scientific materialism cannot afford free will even in principle, they will have to be sceptical of their sciences as well. There are also certain phenomena that are clearly forever beyond our ability to comprehend, like the origin of our cosmos and life and this realization is bound to make them cynical of the sciences too.

Scientism and atheism are antithetical to humanism because both cannot believe in free will and the uniqueness of humanity—for them we are just another species of animals. Humanism minus Christianity is puerile speciesism—no other culture or religion can give a solid foundation to humanism as Christianity can. For example, there was humanistic thought even in other non-Christian cultures like China, India, and even ancient Greece. Ever wondered why humanism did not flourish in those cultures to the extent that it does in Christian nations? This should make it very clear that humanism is lame and puerile without Christianity. Unfortunately, humanism in the west hopes to retain Christian ideals while ignoring Christian beliefs that are the very foundation of those ideals.

We can clearly see danger for humanity in an atheistic world which is morally ambiguous. Perhaps an example will help. Suppose there is an overzealous zoologist, let's call him HH Dawkins Dennett who is so enamoured by nature that he decides to eliminate humans, who he considers as pests that have drastically reduced the biodiversity of the planet. He decides to target

Asia, since that is where the maximum "pests" are located. We want to know which atheist or humanist in the West will step in to confront and stop him? And on what grounds? The atheistic worldview simply has nothing within its framework to stop this mad zoologist.

We have ample historical evidence that this has already happened in the past. Mao Zedong, one of the greatest mass-murderers in the history of mankind, thought such massacres will do well for China by reducing its population. His apathy clearly stems from his ignorance of the gospels.

It is baffling to see the atheists get on the podium and criticize religion. If any injustice is done to a citizen of a country, that citizen can go to the judicial courts for justice. But his arguments must be grounded on the constitution of that country. It cannot be some airy-fairy abstractions like "well-being of sentient beings." One cannot win a legal case in any way, other than referring to the constitution. But atheists have none. It is like challenging a specific code of conduct in a country which has no legal constitution to base its judgements on. It is very clear by this that the atheists are the gun-toting outlaws in this case, who are harassing the law-abiding citizens.

All atheistic criticism of religion is therefore invalid for the following reasons: Firstly, the atheists have no moral foundation (no constitution) to compare and justify their claims. Secondly, they have no room for free will in their materialistic worldview and therefore all their preaching is in direct contradiction to the worldview they hold. It is like preaching to Mister Nitro and Mister Glycerin not to explode when they shake hands—makes no sense. Thirdly, they believe that there is no ultimate meaning or purpose of life. They encourage us to find our own purpose in life. This is kind of absurd if you happen to meet an atheistic pyromaniac with a definitive agenda. Besides, what point is ethics in a pointless world of theirs? Especially for the juvenile down the street who believes in instant gratification. Finally, scientists still have no clue what consciousness is and how our brain functions. It would be disastrous to set the rules for humanity based on such half knowledge.

The atheists are perpetrating the greatest damage to humanity by attempting to destroy our moral foundations in religion without having a replacement ready. Even if they claim to have a replacement, there is currently no universal consensus on any of those. They are only mammon-racking best sellers. Anthony Grayling equates what is good with a good life like the Greeks. Sam Harris and Michael Shermer follow suit by advocating well-being of sentient beings.

Some examples might help to see the absurdity of their ethics. Anthony Grayling in his book *The God Argument* sees nothing wrong with prostitution and the use of drugs. In his skewed worldview, he believes that prostitution saves the institution of marriage. For goodness sake, which planet is this bloke from? Does he have any clue how many families have been destroyed by adultery and drugs?

Many atheists like Christopher Hitchens used to mock believers saying that no one is going to "make out" on the road in the absence of religion or a belief in God. But that is exactly what is happening on the internet. Pornography is being streamed shamelessly to every street corner in the world. Few atheists even go to the most absurd extent and think that they cannot find anything wrong with incest. This is as shocking as it can get!

Another baffling claim the atheists make is that they can also be good people. We don't think so. Atheists not only cannot define what is good, but even if they can, they still cannot be good because their worldview is grounded on scientific materialism which denies them the free will to be good. If they seem to be good, they are just dumb machines programmed to be so. And pray what happens if those machines malfunction?

Even if we set the contradiction of free will aside for a moment, atheists and rationalists are naive enough to think that they can decide what is good through rational consensus. Once we open it up for consensus then the majority wins, irrelevant of whether they are right or wrong. With democracies on the rise worldwide, humanity has indeed begun to decide what is right and wrong through a Gallup poll. What if the Palestinians vote for a party whose manifesto is to destroy Israel? Or if South Africa re-elects a government that has racial discrimination as its core agenda. How will one decide what is good in such cases?

The pandemonium is right before our eyes: a certain country passes a bill to say it is okay to be gay, while a state within that country prohibits it. And to top it all, certain corporates within that state propose "inclusion," saying there should be no discrimination against gays. Who should the employee of that corporate listen to? To the leaders in the corporate, the state in which the corporate is located, or the country in which that state is located? All of whom have contradictory views. Of course, many will happily go with the corporate policy for their own "well-being." But if one thinks they are wrong then on what basis do they think that? On the basis of personal whim? Or the collective whim of a Gallup poll?

Many object to abiding by rules set by God saying divine revelation can be arbitrary. But nothing is further from the truth. In fact, divine revelation is the key to truth precisely because it transcends our own nature. If any analysis has to be objective in nature then it has to transcend it; otherwise, it will be subjective and parochial. Compare that to the carnal revelation of lumbering robots which is always subject to either nature or nurture. The only alternative to "God said so…" is "This lumbering robot said so…" or "This committee of robots with half knowledge says so…" or worse "Mao said so…" In the absence of God, man begins to play God with disastrous consequences. History is rife with such examples and those who do not learn from it are condemned to repeat it.

Unlike many other religions, the Christian revelation was not a secret or private revelation given by an angel in a cave. It was given openly to the whole nation of Israel in public discourses by Christ in flesh and blood. These are divine commandments given openly in public at a definitive place and time in history. There can be nothing arbitrary about such a revelation. What Christ revealed is full and final. We expect no other new revelation. The Church is merely a custodian of this revelation. Even if a new revelation is given, it has to be consistent with what Christ revealed before. Any contradiction is a red flag, an alert that there is something wrong with the new revelation.

Since we adhere to the "Divine Command" theory of morality (as it is labelled in philosophy,) we will need to deal with what is called the Euthyphro dilemma which states: If what is good is objective and independent of God then why do we need Him to tell us what is good? (Is it good because God says so or did God say so because it is objectively good independent of Him?) The atheists claim that humanity can figure out what is good if it is an objective truth independent of God. We think the Euthyphro dilemma resolves favourably in a theistic worldview rather than the atheist one. Atheism based on scientific materialism cannot afford free will and therefore will be unable to judge what is good or bad in an objective way. One would rather take the word of an infinitely wise Creator God than the word of entities who have no free will, whose knowledge is but a drop in an ocean of ignorance, and who don't understand how even their own brain works. It is better for my car to be repaired and fine-tuned by the manufacturers, rather than road side mechanics who conduct experiments on my car at my expense. They neither created me nor do they know me fully, how dare they set the agenda for me?

What then could be the most rational basis of morality? It should be clear to us now that religion can be the only rational foundation. But from the atheist, we hear a deafening silence—or a vague airy fairy "well-being of sentient beings." There is an enlightening verse in the Bible that describes such atheistic morals and ethics: "Having a form of godliness, but denying the power thereof: from such turn away." (2 Timothy 3:5.)

There are therefore two choices kept before mankind.

In a theistic worldview, we can choose divine revelation (Christianity to be specific) as our moral compass. One in which the source is omniscient. In a worldview where the moral framework is an objective truth. One that has room for free will and makes humanity morally responsible. One which says you are a special creation having the ability to chart your own destiny. One which says that there is a special purpose for humanity. All of this in a wonderful cosmos that is amenable to objective scientific enquiry.

In an atheistic worldview, we can choose a carnal revelation that cannot afford any free will. A worldview which is subjective, parochial, and clueless regarding the human condition. One which says you are a lumbering robot without free will and will go on to make you either a guinea pig or a Pavlov's dog depending on who is winning the nature versus nurture debate. One which says there is no ultimate purpose for humanity and believes that their lives are pointless. And one in which concepts of freedom, liberty, and justice are illusory.

The first is constructive and the second is destructive to the human spirit. The first is consistent with science, logic, and rationality and the second is contradictory and self-defeating in all three. The first has hope for mankind and the second has none. The first encourages the spirit of scientific inquiry and the second stifles it. It does not take an Einstein to see which of the above two worldviews is likely to commit crimes against humanity. It does not take a Newton to see which of these worldviews support humanism better. Atheism and scientific materialism are an anathema to the human spirit. The first choice then is the most rational and consistent of the two. Allow us to rephrase a common proverb: a known angel (religion) is better than an unknown devil (atheism.)

On a parting note, we have to deal with historical criticism of religion. We have to admit that the church in history has gone astray many times. But rest assured that we have learned from our past mistakes and have come out wiser. At the same time, we have to be clear that we cannot blame Christianity for everything that the Christians did, especially when what they did was contrary to the code of conduct of the very religion they professed. Merely professing a religion will not do. If I hate my brother then by definition I am not a Christian, no matter what I boast about myself. To be Christian is to follow the precepts laid down by Christ. Going by this definition, Those who persecuted witches and slaves were not Christian, regardless of what they outwardly professed to be. Christ will call them hypocrites just like he called the Scribes and Pharisees of His day. A code of conduct therefore defines a particular religion and strict adherence to it defines the believer.

But the crucial truth we derive from Christianity is that the true enemy of mankind is not religion but the evil nature of man himself. Even the theory of evolution agrees that nature is ruthless and brutal. Charles Caleb wrote nearly two centuries ago that men will kill for their religion, riot for their religion, and even die for their religion but unfortunately will never live by their religion. We should therefore be weary of violence done in the name of a particular religion and instead probe whether it was done according to that particular religion. One cannot blame the constitution because of a few outlaws.

At the same time, being religious does not magically transformed one into a saint overnight. If one were baptized as a Christian and one were to go to church every Sunday, that still does not make one morally perfect in a short while. It will only set the agenda for reform. Currently, it is only Christianity that is emphasizing the evil nature of the fallen man and making the effort to reform him. Don't muzzle the ox while it treads the corn.

Key Summary

It is a mistake to assume like many do, that atheism is equal to secular humanism. It is not. Atheists have no right in staking a claim on humanism, because there is no connecting dot between them. Their worldview is devoid of any moral imperatives and will inevitably end up in nihilism or cynicism. They could even turn out to be communists or Maoists.

Historically, atheists were moral relativists—those who believe that morals are cultural and parochial. In this, they were at least honest in evaluating the consequences of their worldview which was based on scientific materialism and evolution. But somewhere down the line a random mutation seems to have changed them into moral realists—the belief that there are moral absolutes independent of culture. Unfortunately, the new atheists are not even honest in evaluating the consequences of their worldview. The only basis for moral realism can be theism.

Another baffling claim the atheists make is that they can also be good people. But we beg to differ. Atheists not only cannot define what is good but even if they can, they still cannot be good because their worldview is grounded on scientific materialism which denies them the free will to be good. If they seem to be good, they are just dumb machines programmed to be so. And pray what happens if those machines malfunction?

Since we adhere to the "Divine Command" theory of morality (as it is labelled in philosophy) we will need to deal with what is called the Euthyphro dilemma which states: If what is good is objective and independent of God then why do we need Him to tell us what is good? (Is it good because God says so or did God say so because it is objectively good independent of Him?) The atheists claim that humanity can figure out what is good if it is an objective truth independent of God. We think the Euthyphro dilemma resolves favourably in a theistic worldview rather than the atheistic one. Atheism based on scientific materialism cannot afford free will and therefore will be unable to judge what is good or bad in an objective way. One would rather take the word of an infinitely wise Creator God than the word of entities who have no free will, whose knowledge is but a drop in an ocean of ignorance, and who don't understand how even their own brain works. It is better for my car to be repaired and fine-tuned by the manufacturers, rather than road side mechanics who conduct experiments on my car at my expense. They neither created me nor do they know me fully, how dare they set the agenda for me?

What has science got to do with ethics and morality?

Everybody talks about the twin towers these days, but they seem to have conveniently forgotten the twin cities of Hiroshima and Nagasaki. And how a bunch of directionless scientists were drinking and dancing on the success of their new invention—the atom bomb—even as people were dying in those cities. They also conveniently forget how the twin super-powers—USA and former USSR which were empowered by spineless scientists—have brought humanity to the brink of extinction because of the ideological differences they had during the cold war. Those who talk about the local chemist or pharmacist saving lives seem to have forgotten the chemists of Nazi Germany who committed the deadliest genocide in the history of mankind.

While Robert Oppenheimer who led the team that developed the first nuclear bomb openly confessed that scientists have known sin, the militant atheists cherry-pick quotes on the greatest tragedy that has occurred in the history of humankind. Michael Shermer in his book *The Moral Arc* conveniently quotes Jacob Bronowski, who was so enamoured by science that he failed to see anything wrong with it, even after witnessing the devastation which one of the first atom bombs had unleashed. After visiting Nagasaki, he had the audacity to write in his book *Science and Human Values* that "Science has nothing to be ashamed of even in these ruins of Nagasaki." Excuse me? Did I read that right? It is utterly appalling to read something like that. How dare he exonerate science from its guilt?

Many think that science has done a lot of good for humanity. But they do not realize that science has done infinitely more damage to humanity and our planet in the last century than all the religious wars and persecutions have done in the past three millennia. A grim reminder that while science has nothing to do with morality, it is the scientists who need to be browbeaten into a moral framework more than anyone else.

It is quite disturbing to see Lewis Wolpert and Richard Dawkins mock religion by saying that they don't need it to tell them that killing is wrong. If that is so, how come Stalin and Mao (who banished religion from society) did not know that? And went on to massacre millions in the name of their atheistic ideology. How come the chemists at the Nazi camp did not know that? Or the scientists employed in the Manhattan Project? Or those who are currently working in the weapons industry even today? Do they expect their missiles to be used as joy rides for children? Or do they expect their automatic machine guns to be used as harmless toys by big boys?

There are many who will be scandalized by these allegations, but our concern is genuine. Who is to be blamed for the nuclear arsenal that currently exists on the planet, if not the scientists? And where is the conscience of those scientists whose belly is their god? Who governs these scientists across borders? And who monitors their activities? What moral framework are they bound by—provincial or universal? Whom do they obey? Political leaders whose only worry is power or their corporate bosses whose only worry is mammon?

The real danger to humanity then is not religion, but science without a moral compass. Many think science has made religion redundant. We have just seen in the last century what will ensue if that happens. The two world wars had nothing to do with religion, yet caused immense suffering to mankind and large-scale destruction of Europe. All that mayhem was caused by the advance weaponry which scientists had developed without any moral scruples during that period. This should teach us that we ignore religion at our peril.

Does the scientific method have anything in it to make people more humane? Of course not. Does science always work for the good of the society? Not at all. More than half of the scientists in the world are currently working on weapon-related projects which enable large-scale destruction while the rest are working for selfish corporates that have ravaged our planet in order to score high at the stock exchange. In such a scenario, scientists are the ones who are in urgent need of moral reformation. It is abundantly clear to us that they are not getting their morality from either science or from popular paperbacks written by Grayling, Shermer, or Harris.

Scientists are the true terrorists here, terrorizing innocent citizens throughout the world with their crooked devices. I don't think anyone can forget what the Napalm bombs have done to innocent children in Vietnam. We don't think the blame can go to anyone other than the scientists. On one hand, they say that humans are genetically modified apes and robots programmed by their genome to ruthlessly survive, and on the other, put lethal bombs into their hands. Don't the scientists talk to each other? Does the weapons expert not speak to the anthropologist or the evolutionist to discuss the repercussions of developing such powerful weapons of mass destruction? On one hand, they say that we cannot have free will and on the other hand they put guns into their hands under the guise of personal freedom and liberty. On one hand, they criticize the politicians and on the other, build deadly weapons for them under the guise of deterrence. But who are they deterring? The politician on the other side with his own battery of scientists?

If scientists are atheists then the danger is manifold. Atheistic China jumped to editing the genome of humans without any moral qualms as soon as the CRISPR-cas9 technology was available to them. Who or what is going to stop such atheistic scientists across countries? We are sure US and Europe will soon dive into it because they don't want to be left behind in science. In this rat race, humanity itself will be at peril. And when scientists like James Watson make outrageous statements like: "But then, in all honesty, if scientists don't play god, who will?" then the danger for humanity is manifold.

Science needs governance more than any other institution on the planet and we can no longer trust the politicians to oversee this. In fact, ideological and economic interests are the primary reasons that provide impetus to develop weapons of mass destruction. They are also easily influenced by corporates (who fund their campaigns and lobby to have their way) who have ravaged the planet earth for selfish gain and have supplied countless destructive weapons to third-world nations thereby creating unprecedented chaos and suffering in those nations. We cannot trust philosophers because they hardly ever agree with each other on anything and are equally influenced by local ideologies. We cannot trust science because it is bound by its materialistic worldview that denies free will needed to make one morally responsible.

We already have empirical evidence on how a secular institution devoid of religion fails ethically in spite of their grandiose claims on science and rationality. It is called a university, and we know what a disaster it has been. Firstly, by asserting that God should be kept out, they are ignoring astounding empirical evidence for the existence of God like the fine-tuning of the universe and the complexity found in a simple living cell. As a result, they are not going where the evidence is leading them, but instead are becoming increasingly dogmatic in their materialistic assertions. If they were sincere in their quest for truth without their atheistic bias, they would be the ones who would be leading revival meetings in Churches.

Secondly, the universities gladly accept funding without any moral scruples. Universities help research and arm their countries with weapons of mass destruction. They also help corporates to rake a quick buck by ravaging the resources on our planet. The important question is who governs these universities and what moral code are they following? Who will bell this cat before it becomes a mad tiger which we will no longer be able to ride? We don't see any humanists around there. Who is reviewing the performance of the scientists from the ethics perspective? Occasionally, governments intervene and govern the universities in their respective countries. But if the government itself is rudderless (secular) like the university and is driven by politicians who dance to the tune of the majority or to the tune of corporates who influence public policy for money, we can clearly see the clouds of dystopia gathering over such nations.

If the atheists are so worried about this world, they should be preaching first to these scientists and researchers who are working in the weapons industry and mammon seeking corporates. This is proverbial picking the speck in their brothers' (religion) eye while ignoring the log in their own. Blind science has not only empowered humanity to self-destruct but is bringing all the ecological biodiversity to the brink of extinction for selfish gain. Humanity itself which is empowered by science needs religion more than ever to guide it. The more ethically grounded we are, the safer our science will be. What we currently need is not scientific progress but a moral reformation.

We should therefore stop all research in science until we get a clear commitment to a moral framework from the scientists. We highly recommend that they choose Christianity, the only religion that preaches love, peace, and forbearance to all humanity. One in which humans are a special creation made in the image of God. Not the religions of the east, where one can be reborn in the animal or plant kingdom, nor secular humanism which believes that man is just another species of animal.

Almost all scientists and philosophers agree that science cannot have anything to say about values. Of course, science can help us make informed decisions if we give it a specific objective to attain like the well-being of humanity. Where those objectives come from is the key.

Just like scientific reductionism which relapses into an infinite regress of cause and effect, moral statements also become a *reductio ad absurdum* of "why" questions unless an ultimate purpose or objective is defined. Science and atheism have no such objective or purpose to offer mankind. To circumvent this problem, many atheists encourage us to find our own purpose. But it is easy to see that any moral code based on a personal agenda relapses into moral relativism and we cannot have a common code of conduct to resolve conflicting moral statements. If it is not "God said so" then it will either be a whimsical "I said so" or "you said so" or "we said so." Since science cannot frame an ethical framework, the constitution of a country then must necessarily be based on religion—we highly recommend Christianity for reasons that will crystallize in the chapters to come.

Every atheistic attempt to construct a moral framework is fraught with inconsistencies and contradictions. There is no point in setting the agenda for entities that in their view have no room for free will. They profess moral realism which ought to be objective yet they depend on subjective experimental results. They appeal to moral intuitions, common sense, and an innate conscience which makes sense only when I am made in the image of God and not in the image of an ape. They advocate the well-being of individual sentient beings, but their books are full of statistics based on research done on groups of people (which is more relevant to utilitarian ethics.) None of the experiments mentioned in their books have been repeated globally to see if it applies to every culture. What if the results are different? Will there be a different ethical system for every culture on the planet? A relapse to moral relativism is inevitable in such a scenario.

The militant atheists are completely isolated and deluded in thinking that science can determine human values even as the consensus in the academia is quite the opposite. We have seen in the earlier chapter that science is a method of discovery that tells us how things work and not dictate how we ought to behave. It will therefore have nothing to do with ethics or morality. No equation in science or math can derive objectives like "love your neighbour as yourself." Many atheistic scientists including Sean Carroll and Jerry Coyne know this and have openly confessed that science has nothing to say about ethics and morals. In fact, Sean Carroll put it aptly when he said that claiming to derive a moral framework from science is like claiming they got an odd number by adding up two even numbers—which is mathematically and rationally impossible. Noble laureate Steven Weinberg says it is "absolute nonsense" that people think science can determine human values. Atheists need to convince their own comrades before setting out to change the world.

In direct contradiction to scientific and philosophical consensus, Sam Harris writes in his book *The Moral Landscape* that science can decide on a moral framework. We have to remember that his book is not a scientific or philosophical paper that has been peer-reviewed. Their view reeks of double standards. We can clearly see parallels between their claims and the claims of those who promote alternative medicine like acupuncture and homeopathy that have their own set of rules and principles which are totally different from mainstream science and medicine.

Their sophistry is even more evident when it comes to dealing with the problem of free will. In trying to wriggle out of this problem, they invent the third greatest oxymoron mankind has known, "deterministic free will," a concept that no scientist will agree for obvious reasons and yet has a following within the atheistic camp for even more obvious reasons. In the current scenario, it is quite evident that scientists disagree among themselves and philosophers disagree among themselves and both scientists and philosophers disagree with each other on concepts such as free will and ethics.

The moral landscape as envisaged by Sam Harris is nothing more than a map of what is "pleasurable" because there is no scientific metric for joy and happiness. If we try to map joy and happiness then the results will be very subjective and we will eventually relapse into moral relativism. More importantly, doing what feels good for us might not always reflect the right thing to do. In fact, our zeal for well-being is putting the entire planet at risk. In such a scenario, we will have to sacrifice our well-being for future generations. Which equation in science can tell us that?

Taking drugs would be a peak in the "moral landscape" of Harris, but is it the right thing to do? In our quest to end suffering completely, suppose we rig our neural-system to always give pleasurable sensations—even when pinched—to the extent that people are giggling at funerals. Would the distinction between good and bad vanish?

No matter how we see it, there will always be one crucial contradiction in the moral landscape of Harris. Whose well-being is he talking about? If it is individual well-being as Shermer and Harris envisage it to be, then everywhere in the world, every individual is doing exactly that—ensuring his or her own well-being. They do not need books or lectures from atheists to tell them that. The real problem is when my peak becomes my neighbour's deepest valley. One person's dream can become another person's nightmare. There are many such situations in the world. Palestinian peak will be a valley for Israel. North Korean peak will be the deepest valley for the south. Science or atheism have nothing in their worldview to resolve such scenarios. It takes the Bible to tell us to love our neighbours as ourselves and work towards their well-being and make this world a better place.

Of course, there are many places in the world where it is not that obvious to their citizens that the well-being of every individual is paramount. Islamic nations and their treatment of women, India's caste system in the rural areas and China's one-child policy are a few primary examples. While atheists are preaching from their ivory towers, it is the Christian missionaries who are on the ground and doing their best by sacrificing their own "well-being" to bring about a change. Why don't the atheists convert to Christianity and join the forces? After all, did Dawkins not come up with the concept of "Atheists for Jesus" because he found Jesus to be "super nice?" And did not the icon of physics Albert Einstein have high regard for Christ when he confessed that "No man, can deny the fact that Jesus existed, nor that his sayings are beautiful. Even if some of them have been said before, no one has expressed them so divinely as he."

Sam Harris claims that even truth can be sacrificed for well-being. He thinks it is okay to lie in order to save lives. Taking an example of lying to the Nazi perpetrators in order to save the lives of a few Jews hidden in the cellar. By doing this, he is opening a Pandora's Box. I am not sure if he will be okay when a concerned mother tells him that she does not want the theory of evolution taught in schools for the well-being of her child. Which parent wants the school to teach their children concepts like survival of the fittest? Will Sam Harris advocate banning the teaching of evolution in schools?

Unfortunately, there are obdurate atheists like Peter Atkins who go a step further in asserting that philosophy (where ethics is studied) and religion (the source of ethics) have no value. This is a dangerous predicament. Where do the scientists plan to get their moral framework from in such a scenario? Since knowledge is power, science needs religion for guiding it to use its scientific knowledge with prudence and empathy. Without religion, science is like an ape unleashed inside a glass factory.

Half knowledge is nowhere more dangerous than here. Science is currently clueless about how to resolve the "hard problem" of consciousness and how it relates to free will. Although Benjamin Libet's experiments show that we may not have free will while making quick decisions, we do not know for certain if that extends to long term decisions or goals as well—whether one is hard wired to be a saint or a criminal. Indeed, Libet himself argued that there was still room for a veto over a decision that may have been made unconsciously without free will. There is currently no consensus on free will even among the scientists. It is clear to us that consciousness and free will are intertwined; we cannot resolve the latter without resolving the former. Dawkins and Hitchens avoid this question using humour, which is not at all funny considering the importance of this question. Science should first resolve these problems of consciousness and free will before jumping the gun on ethics. It would be foolish to set an agenda without knowing the true nature of our mind. Otherwise, it will be a textbook case of blind leading the blind.

Partial scientific knowledge in the hands of scientific materialists and atheists is very dangerous, especially when you are a "nobody" in their view. They assert that your consciousness is a pointless sensation of the brain and insist that your mind equals to your material brain. They assert that you are a genetically modified ape, a robot constructed by your genes to ruthlessly survive. They assert that you cannot have free will. They assert that your life is pointless in a purposeless universe. Wonder what "values" can ever come forth from such a worldview as theirs?

Whether the theory of evolution is right or wrong is a separate question, but like any scientific theory, it can and has influenced the ethics of our society in the past. History testifies how cut-throat American capitalism became after the phrase "survival of the fittest" was coined. Even worse was the Holocaust, which was the direct consequence of the Nazi concept of a pure race and its experiment with eugenics, a term coined by Darwin's half-cousin Francis Galton. We shudder at what could have happened if it turned out that the genome of Africans was inferior to that of the Caucasian or if the brains of women turned out to be inferior to men. A society which is so enamoured by science would probably end up treating them both as menial slaves.

Nature and nurture debates have been going on forever without any resolution in sight. But it is obvious what the atheists believe in. Michael Shermer believes that a brain tumour can cause one to be a paedophile. At which point, I am not sure how they can criticize religion. Maybe the Islamic jihadi has a unique configuration in his brain or a bit of sand from the Arabian desert got into his brain! Given such a materialistic worldview of the atheists, even if they agree on a moral framework, they will implement it by making humanity either guinea pigs or Pavlov's dogs based on who wins the nature versus nurture debate. We are not sure what freedom, liberty, and justice they can proclaim for humanity in such a scenario.

Who then decides how we should behave? It is inevitable that the entity which created us decides on how we ought to behave. If it is the monotheistic God of Abraham, then it is His prerogative to set the agenda for mankind. If it is "nothing but" matter and laws of physics then those materialistic forces will set the agenda for mankind, irrespective of what the atheists want to believe.

In the latter scenario, free will is an illusion and all our rational debates are delusions. But in the former worldview in which humanity is created in the image of God, we have the foundations of freedom, liberty, and justice. How dare then we keep our Creator God out of the public sphere? In fact, He should be central in all our plans and activities as a society.

There is no one else who can take the place of our Creator. Not the atheists who are amoral, not the scientific materialists, since they cannot even in principle believe in free will. Not the secular humanists who blindly believe in what science tells them (that we are chemical scum.) Not the politicians whose agenda is power. Not the philosophers who can never agree among themselves on anything. Not the congregation of lumbering robots (in the atheistic worldview) called a democracy where the majority wins instead of what is true or right. Either our Creator God or the materialistic forces of nature will set the agenda, whether we like it or not. Fall in line or get out of the way.

Key Summary

The real danger to humanity is not religion, but science without a moral compass. Many think science has made religion redundant. We have just seen in the last century what will ensue if that happens. The two world wars had nothing to do with religion, yet caused immense suffering to mankind and large-scale destruction of Europe. All that mayhem was caused by the advance weaponry which scientists had developed without any moral scruples during that period. This should teach us that we ignore religion at our peril.

Science needs governance more than any other institution on the planet and we can no longer trust the politicians to oversee this. In fact, ideological and economic interests are the primary reasons that provide impetus to develop weapons of mass destruction. They are also easily influenced by corporates (who fund their campaigns and lobby to have their way) who have ravaged the planet earth for selfish gain and have supplied countless destructive weapons to third-world nations thereby creating unprecedented chaos and suffering in those nations. We cannot trust philosophers because they hardly ever agree with each other on anything and are equally influenced by local ideologies. We cannot trust science because it is bound by its materialistic worldview that denies free will needed to make one morally responsible.

We should therefore stop all research in science until we get a clear commitment to a moral framework from the scientists. We highly recommend that they choose Christianity, the only religion that preaches love, peace, and forbearance to all humanity. One in which humans are a special creation made in the image of God. Not the religions of the east, where one can be reborn in the animal or plant kingdom, nor secular humanism which believes that man is just another species of ape.

WHY WE NEED RELIGION NOW
MORE THAN EVER

If we define religion not only as a belief in God but also one which has a code of conduct then we see no reason for religion to be redundant. Any society where it is taboo to point out its moral deficiencies is heading for dystopia. Religion has always been the conscience keeper of societies and nations. The churches in the west are empty not because they are lacking something, but because it demands a change in lifestyle. Unfortunately, that is exactly what is difficult for the present generation that has been brought up worshipping the Statue of Liberty as their mother goddess. Reason why we see moral degradation in schools, in universities, in politics, and in the general society. We must remember that freedom comes with a responsibility.

Every society and nation needs a constitution—a rule book of sorts—to govern it. Otherwise it will be like driving on roads without rules or traffic lights. Utter pandemonium will ensue. Many atheists boast at the progress made by the Scandinavian countries without religion. Unfortunately, such naïve conclusions are the result of staring at the statistical tables in their ivory towers while blithely ignoring the ground reality. Amsterdam is a lawless jungle after dark with the police helplessly giving up on patrolling in the nights. This is a textbook example of how the dangerous concoction of unbridled freedom and drugs can lead to a collapse in law and order.

Having an ethical framework is only the first step. The second part is to have a committee that is the custodian of that framework. The true enemies of mankind are those religions, institutions, and societies that have no central committee to nurture that responsibility.

Most Christian denominations have a steering committee that is bound by ethics formulated by Christ alone. The Catholics have the Vatican while the protestant denominations have their own. One can steer the whole of Christendom by appealing to their steering committees. Contrast that with Islam and Hinduism. Even though both have their own ethical frameworks, they have no steering committee. No single body can steer the whole of Islam or Hinduism in the right direction.

The situation is even more dangerous in science. We have no control over what scientists do since they don't have any central governing body that transcends nations. Every scientist is either a slave of his own country, developing destructive weapons for it, or a slave of rich corporates that pay him to exploit our planet. If scientists in America decide to stop development of nuclear weapons, the Chinese scientists may not respond in the same way as their American counterparts because there is no central governing body in science that transcends governments and corporates. No one has the power or authority to stop science from doing something which can be detrimental to our planet. This is a dangerous predicament.

With the power of science at hand, a code of conduct for the scientists is more important than anything else in the world. If there are any entities that should be closely scrutinized, then those should be the universities of the world. Because it is in the universities that science is taught without moral obligations. Such research is used by their respective countries to either boost national pride or for selfish gain of corporates. We have learned from experience that both of them are detrimental for humaity. The armament industry is a perfect example of that. Science without a moral compass is a clear and present danger for humanity.

The crucial question is who defines the code of conduct? Atheists who are amoral and directionless and insist that the universe is pointless? Politicians who are power mongers? Corporates who seek selfish gain? Scientists who deny free will? Or humanists who blindly believe what science tells them? The problem should be obvious to all. Of all the worldviews, a theistic worldview is self-consistent and the rational choice because it believes that we have free will to be morally responsible in a universe that has a definitive purpose. Compare that to the atheistic worldview: what point is ethics in a pointless world of theirs? Currently, there are more people committing suicide than dying of war and disease. A grim warning of how a purposeless society will turn out to be in the future.

"Religion is the opium of the masses" said Karl Marx. Why not use this for the benefit of humanity? Why reinvent the wheel? It is already widespread and has a presence at the grass-root level. Christianity has the potential to be a great unifier across nations, ideologies, and geography. It can help science frame a common ethical framework that every scientist in the world should follow, irrespective of what form of government is ruling them, which country they are residing in, and what the ideology of their country is. Only if all the scientists throughout the world strictly abide by Christian principles and refuse to blindly follow what politicians and corporates are telling them (if they are against humanity) can we have some hope of ending pointless suffering in the world.

In history, there is plenty of evidence on the positive role played by religion. Humanity has to thank religion for civilizing it. Ara Norenzayan says that without religion, humanity would still be in stone ages (New Scientist: "God Issue: Religion is the key to civilization," dated March 2012.) Thankfully many atheists agree that Christianity has done immense good for humanity. But it is baffling to see Richard Dawkins deny that. Instead, he thinks it is culture that we have to thank. Does this bloke have any idea how local cultures pose the main obstacle for a universal ethical system? Has he even considered how inhumane certain cultures in the world are? According to the cultures of Africa and Papua New Guinea, there was nothing wrong with cannibalism. In India, it was considered virtuous for a widowed woman to join the funeral pyre of her husband and be burned alive. We can give countless such examples of dangerous practices throughout the world and all these cultural practices were blithely going on until the Christian missionaries arrived in those countries. Even the savage pre-Christian cultures of Europe like the Vikings and Visigoths were great impediments for the spread of Christianity. After Christianity established itself in Europe, local cultures and superstitions continued to corrupt the Church and made it depart from the essential teachings of Christ many times. Clear example of how local cultures make ethical systems parochial, subjective, and downright dangerous. It took a religion like Christianity to bring about a universal ethical system and unite mankind across races, cultures, and nations.

Research also points out that even the current secular nations of Europe— especially the Scandinavian countries—have used Christianity to move up the ethical ladder and later let it go. Anyone who has elementary knowledge of European history knows very well how Christianity transformed the barbaric continent into a more sensible one that it is now. The world must thank Christian missionaries for transforming Europe, which went on to transform the entire world.

We should also thank God because Christianity came before science to Europe. Imagine the plight of our planet if the Vikings and Visigoths had the technology to create nuclear weapons! It would have been sheer pandemonium. In fact, mankind would have long gone extinct if science preceded Christianity.

Both science and religion profess to pursue objective truths and therefore cannot admit to any kind of plurality. Science deals with truths of nature and religion with truths of morality and ethics. The only challenge for both of them is how to deal with falsity. Even science does not tolerate falsity. No one in the university advocates that alchemy should to be taught in schools. Why then should religion tolerate false premises of ethics and morality?

The crucial question then is which religion or moral framework should we follow? We would argue that Christianity is the only viable religion in today's world. There are many reasons for us to believe that, but if one does not agree then we are open to a sincere debate on this. In the interim, if we have to debate and yet be tolerant of other religions, then Christianity alone is the answer with its doctrine of forbearance and forgiveness as preached by Christ. No other religion has a better way of dealing with falsity while on a quest for ultimate truth.

It will be evident to all who read the Gospels that violence and judgement are a strict no-no. For a true Christian, there can be only three kinds of people in this world. Those who know the truth and have accepted it: we have fellowship with them. Those who do not know the truth: we preach to them. And finally, those who know the truth but have rejected it: we pray for them and occasionally debate with them. Christianity in its essence is both tolerant and uncompromising on truth, unlike Islam which is not tolerant of other religions and Hinduism which compromises on truth by admitting to a plurality.

It is true that the Church has violated the fundamental precepts of Christianity and has gone astray many a time, but these are mistakes that we should learn from. Any criticism of Christianity therefore, should call for reformation and not elimination because the former is constructive while the latter is destructive. The clergy might have failed us, but Jesus Christ—the author and finisher of our faith—will never fail us. To give up religion just because a few clergymen have failed us, is like giving up on the constitution and deciding to be outlaws just because of a few corrupt officials. Nothing can be more counterproductive. Instead, we need to reinforce our commitment to Christianity and pray for the clergy and encourage them in their difficult ministry. The clergy may not be infallible, but they are least likely to be wrong in the same way a doctor, an engineer, or a lawyer are least likely to be wrong in their respective fields.

It is also true that believers themselves have set a bad example at times. But before the atheists make blanket statements and criticize all religions, they should examine if violence has been done according to a certain religion rather than in the name of that religion. Under no circumstances is violence allowed in Christianity—Christ Himself set a brilliant example for us. The important fact is that it is the re-examination of Christian ethics itself that leads us to condemn what has been wrongly done in God's name in the past. Any reform like Protestantism therefore can only come from within, in the same way that any amendment of a constitution has to be consistent with the existing norms. The atheists have no foundation to base their criticism of religion on, other than their own whim or popular opinion. In this, they are no better than politicians who cleverly create a manifesto based on popular opinion to garner votes.

It is imperative then to educate our children in ethics and morality before imparting scientific knowledge. And currently the only place they can learn that is in the Church—in their Sunday school and youth fellowships. Knowledge is power and power without a moral compass spells disaster for humanity. It should also be mandatory that all admissions into a university have an Hippocratic Oath of sorts, that they will never help develop weapons or further the selfish ambitions of corporates. This will ensure that science will be safe and harmless to our society.

Of course, there will be many objections from the atheistic camp for mandating the above. A common excuse for not believing in divine revelation is the claim that it will be arbitrary. What if some quack claims another quirky revelation? Should we believe that? Of course not.

Unlike many other religions, Jesus Christ was a historical person who gave us this ethical framework to follow. Atheists don't seem to understand that in Christianity the canon is closed. No other revelation will be given apart from what has been revealed by Jesus. His Word is full and final. Saint Paul says that even if an angel were to come and reveal something contrary to what has already been revealed, we have to reject it (Galatians 1:8.) Reason why we don't believe in the revelation given to Mohammed (or Joseph Smith) even if it was from Gabriel or any other angel.

Another common objection that the atheists have regarding religion is that it is not open to revision. They go on to claim that science is better because it has no authority and is open to revision. This is a flawed argument. Science is humanity's attempt to understand nature and therefore should be always open to revision, but we can never open the scientific method itself for revision. Religion therefore cannot be open-ended precisely because it is the very foundation of scientific and rational inquiry. A few examples might help: the Christian injunction to speak only the truth and nothing but the truth, and the verification principle (that the testimony of two witnesses is mandatory to prove a truth claim) can never be open to revision. Both these injunctions are central to science: to speak the truth and to verify that truth by repeating the experiment in another laboratory. It would be disastrous to say that science can occasionally lie to serve the interests of corporates. I am sure the fellows who cooked up the Piltdown hoax did not go to Sunday school, or even if they did, they don't seem to have payed attention to what was being taught. Religion gives us a firm moral foundation to be truthful in scientific inquiry and therefore cannot be open-ended.

Even if we open up religion for revision, we would like to know on what basis would they want to revise it? We have already seen that the atheists are amoral and have no definition of what is right and wrong. Should we then revise religion on the basis of the whim of a genetically modified ape? Isn't that what they believe we are? A lumbering robot that has no free will and has no clue how its own brain works? Or one which has no clue what ninety-five percent of the universe comprises of? Utter disaster awaits humanity if they have confidence in such entities to drive their ethics department.

Even if we overlook all the above fundamental contradictions, we would still like to know what the atheists want to revise in a religion like Christianity.

"Thou shalt not kill" to "go ahead and drop that H-bomb?" or maybe "Thou shalt not bear false witness" to "go ahead and make another Piltdown hoax?" We are very sure that there will be different opinions even among the atheists when we open up the Bible for revision. Some will be pro-life and others pro-choice. Some will be utilitarian while others would disagree. How then do we resolve these different opinions?

Even if one disagrees on a few injunctions mentioned in the Bible, there is no reason to dump Christianity as a whole. It is like dumping the whole constitution just because one does not agree with a few injunctions found in it. Nothing can be more counterproductive. We now know with firsthand experience that opening religion to revision is opening a Pandora's Box, a slippery slope to the depths of chaos and confusion.

The slope is steep indeed. Once we let go off religion then the house is open for justifying everything in the name of freedom and liberty. Consider how casual nudity has become in this generation. Don't trust our judgement on this, even if you bring atheists from the 1800's to the streets today, they would be shocked and dismayed at the way we dress. Or consider the violence in the video games. If you bring a child from the 1800's and make him play a video game today, he would be devastated for life. He would be having nightmares for the rest of his life when he sees the graphic violence and the grotesque imagery that the games depict these days. Or consider what would happen to a child from the 1800's when he watches pornography on the internet! Or if he comes to know that extra-marital affairs are encouraged by a portal on the internet. Everything that is casual these days was shocking in the 1800's, what other empirical evidence does one need to prove the slippery slope?

What we need is a moral reformation. This applies not only to the common man, but also to scientists and politicians before our society relapses into a dystopia. We can clearly see the effects of secular science and politics in the way our planet is exploited and how weapons of mass destruction are manufactured and sold without any control.

Focusing and asserting too much on freedom, liberty, and well-being will always be an obstacle to true moral progress. We should stop making the Statue of Liberty an idol that we must always bow to. While humanity is free to do whatever it wants, not everything it does will be meaningful. An athlete gives up her freedom and liberty to undergo gruelling training along with a disciplined diet because she wants to achieve something more meaningful. Even the army is strictly disciplined because its objective is to protect the citizens. While citizens are free to own as many fuel-guzzling SUVs as they want, they have to sacrifice their freedom and liberty if they want to save our planet. In the same way, God has a great vision for mankind and has set the way before us to achieve it. Even if it means that we give up our freedom, liberty, and well-being in the short run to achieve something greater. If we have such a Biblical perspective, then all our suffering will seem a light affliction. "All things are lawful for me, but all things are not expedient: all things are lawful for me, but all things edify not." (1 Corinthians 10:23.)

The evidence of the transformative power of Christianity is right in front of us to see. The real miracles of Christianity are those that changed individuals, societies, and nations. It changed the vile Augustine to Saint Augustine and murderous Saul to Saint Paul. It also transformed the barbaric Europe into a Holy Roman Empire through which the entire world was transformed. Thankfully, many atheists agree that Christianity transformed the world's civilizations. What else could one ask of a religion?

Steven Weinberg might be a great physicist, but his sense of history is pathetic. We should therefore rephrase him: For bad people to do good things, that takes religion—Christianity to be specific.

Both Christopher Hitchens and Lawrence Krauss say that they would not like to be ruled by a celestial despot. What they don't know is that the God of Christianity is no celestial despot but wants us to be co-heirs of His creation. If the atheists still insist on calling God a despot, then who cares of what they think? Whether they like the current president or not, the fact of the matter is that they are ruled by him. Nobody is here to discuss preferences; they can go to the local pub to do that. As pointed out earlier, it is either our Creator God or the laws of physics and chemistry that govern us. In a materialistic worldview of theirs which believes in bottom-up order, there can be no free will. If both Hitchens and Krauss don't prefer God to rule their lives, they are still slaves of their genome and to the laws of nature whether they like it or not.

Richard Dawkins in his book *Science in the Soul* thinks we should do away with the tyranny of texts (that of the genome and the Bible) and chart our own course since we cherry-pick what is "good" from them anyway. But this is exactly what one should avoid if there are objective truths in ethics. We believe that we should accept truth as it is, whether it is our selfish genome (which tells us who we are) or the New Testament (which tells us how we ought to be.) Just as we go about pursuing science accepting the phenomena as it is and not how we whimsically want them to be, we should cease from fiddling the texts based on our subjective whims. One tells us of our fallen nature and the other the glorious purpose for which mankind was created. Any cherry-picking will render the entire enterprise whimsical.

Key Summary

If we define religion not only as a belief in God but also as one which has a code of conduct then we see no reason for religion to be redundant. Any society where it is taboo to point out its moral deficiencies is heading for dystopia. Religion has always been the conscience keeper of societies and nations. Unfortunately, the current generation has made the Statue of Liberty as their idol and indiscriminate freedom as their personal religion. Reason why we see moral degradation in schools, in universities, in politics, and in the general society. We must remember that freedom comes with a responsibility.

The crucial question then is which religion or moral framework should we follow? We would argue that Christianity is the only viable religion in today's world. There are many reasons for us to believe that, but if one does not agree then we are open to a sincere debate on this. In the interim, if we have to debate and yet be tolerant of other religions, then Christianity alone is the answer with its doctrine of forbearance and forgiveness as preached by Christ. No other religion has a better way of dealing with falsity while on a quest for ultimate truth.

Having an ethical framework is only the first step. The second part is to have a committee that is the custodian of that framework. The true enemies of mankind are those religions, institutions, and societies that have no central committee to nurture that responsibility. Unfortunately, science has no central committee to oversee it. Science therefore is a clear and present danger for humanity. It is like an ape unleashed in a glass factory.

WHICH GOD OR RELIGION?

Which God? This question is often asked by every atheist as if it is some kind of ultimate gotcha, not realizing that atheism is infinitely more ambiguous than religion. We have already shown that humanism has nothing to do with atheism. Atheists could be cynics, nihilists, communists, or Maoists. Some are moral relativists while others are moral realists. Some believe in free will while the majority of them deny it. Some think science can determine human values while others deny that it can do so.

There is ambiguity even in science. Sometimes there are multiple and contradictory theories that contend to explain a given phenomenon. As an example, there have been more theories and worldviews than the hair on my head which attempt to explain the "hard problem" of consciousness. Does that mean consciousness does not exist? That is being totally absurd. Or take the example of quantum physics. There are many who stand by the Copenhagen interpretation while others by the Austin interpretation. Some believe that reality does not exist at the subatomic level until it is measured, while others believe there are infinite parallel universes. Add to this confusion is another interpretation of John Wheeler—that of a participatory universe.

The great chain of delusion should be obvious to everyone by now: the neurologists think the biologists have it figured out, while the biologists think the chemists have it figured out, and the chemists think the physicists have it figured out, little realizing that the physicists have abandoned camp in the last century itself when they encountered the quantum phenomena. In such a situation, science cannot even claim to know what the fundamental nature of reality is. There are multiple interpretations but no consensus even among the physicists. Which reality is science talking about then? In the same way, it is a *non sequitur* to claim that the nature of God cannot be known just because there have been multiple attempts by humans to understand the mind of God. Just as in science, this is a failure of our intellect and not the phenomenon itself.

If they want us to abandon religion just because there are so many in the world, then why not abandon physics because there are so many interpretations to resolve the quantum conundrum? Why not abandon neurosciences because there are so many different opinions regarding consciousness? How come a difference of opinion in science is seen as a virtue, and in religion it is seen as a vice? It is high time that they settle their domestic squabbles first—about quantum physics—before pointing fingers at their neighbours.

Science is also a work in progress that is trying to understand the ultimate nature of reality. We have shown earlier that although science may not vary in geography, it has varied tremendously in time. From claiming that earth, water, air, and fire are the basic elements to the standard model of atomic physics that is currently accepted today—it has been a long journey for science. And the standard model of atomic physics is certainly not a complete and perfect revelation of reality because there are many things that it has yet to answer. In the same way, no religion may have a fully accurate representation of God, but at least one will be a good working model. We should treat every religion in the same way that we treat any scientific and rational framework which is attempting to understand the mind of God. And just like any one theory qualifies in the end, we believe only one religion to be closest to truth—Christianity.

Since most Eastern religions which are not ethical monotheistic believe in a plurality of truth (that all roads lead to the ultimate truth), their worldview cannot afford to have objective moral truths. Such moral ambiguity leads to a "anything goes" attitude. Reason why some of the Eastern nations are the most corrupt in the world.

While all the religions of the world are sincere quests of man trying to understand the mind of God, the Abrahamic religions—Jewish and Christian—have the revelations of God given to mankind. Christ being the fullest revelation of God. We can show many reasons why Christianity is unique among other major religions in the world, but this book is not against other religions, but against atheism. One book we recommend on this topic is *Jesus Among Other Gods* by Ravi Zacharias.

As honest seekers of truth we should eliminate all those religions that are based on myths. By doing that, we eliminate almost all of them, barring a handful. Among the historical ones found in the world only the ethical monotheistic religions stand apart from the others. It is a form of exclusive monotheism in which God is the source for one standard of morality and who guides humanity through ethical principles.

Even among the ethical monotheistic ones, only in Christianity is there a zeal for truth and tolerance of falsity (without resorting to violence or judgement.) With its unique concepts of the unity of humanity, together with forgiveness and forbearance, Christianity becomes the most practical and livable religion on the planet if everyone adheres to its percepts dilligently. I have yet to meet someone whose heart was not stirred by the Sermon on the Mount given by Jesus Christ (Gospel of Matthew chapter 5.) It would have brought the likes of Mullah Omar to seek repentance, if only they had read it.

When comparing religions, we could go on arguing until the cows come home because every religion has its proud moments and its embarrassing moments. Some believers set a good example and some don't. Every religion has its extremist elements too. It is very important therefore that we distinguish between what is done in the name of their religion and what is done according to their religion. This is very crucial when we do a comparative analysis of religions. Many embarrassing things have been done in the name of religion by the Klu Klux Klan, but a casual glance at the Gospels will show that it has been done in direct contradiction to the religion they profess. Instead of cherry-picking or quote mining the good or the bad parts, we should empirically look at what kind of societies that any given religion has nurtured in the long term.

Christ brilliantly gave another measure of verifying a true prophet. "Wherefore by their fruits ye shall know them." (Matthew 7:20.) We can clearly see what kind of fruits various religions of the world are bearing. No one in their right mind would ever want to settle down in the Middle East which is ruled by Islamic orthodoxy. The same can be said of the Hindu caste divisions in rural India. And there is no counting as to how many in atheistic China desperately want to make it to the United States. A clear indication that their religions (or lack of it) are untenable in the long run and the fruits they have given are often very sad and unfortunate for those societies. Only Christianity has stood the test of time and has within it the doctrines of freedom, liberty, justice, and forbearance that mankind is searching for.

Another point that the atheists usually highlight is that many blindly follow the religion that they have been born into. This is again a self-defeating argument. Since atheism itself could be the result of growing up in a godless family or a secular society. Besides, these are lazy arguments in this day and age of internet. While it is true that those who are not passionate about truth will continue in the religion that they are born in, it is baseless to say that none of them are true. One has to diligently seek out the right one and not be lazy.

For example, I have been taught in school that life may have arisen in a warm little pond. If I were not passionate and continued to blithely believe what was taught in school then I would deserve to be called a blind believer. Instead, when I examined the truth on the origin of life, I was totally convinced that there was no way life could have crawled out of a warm little pond. To me intelligent causation was obvious and I stuck to it.

I was born in a city once ruled by Muslim kings, in a state which had ancient history of Buddhism and in a country which is primarily Hindu. When I grew up, I had friends who were Muslims, Hindus, Jains, Parsees, Sikhs, and atheists too. Many have freely converted from one religion to the other and are not necessarily following the religion they are born into. I thank God that my forefathers had the courage to go where evidence and truth led them and ended up choosing Christianity even if it came with a severe social stigma—because it was then believed that Christianity was the religion of the lower castes.

If that is not enough, my wife while she was working in Beijing came across a woman from the remotest place on earth called Tibet, a hardcore Buddhist centre. To my wife's utter disbelief, the woman boldly professed that the true way was Christianity and that she too was a follower of Christ.

Ironically, in India and China, it is the converts who have the fire in their belly to evangelize. One needs to travel to non-Christian nations to see this. In China, the pastors travel thousands of kilometres to attend or lead underground revival meetings. We already know the missionary work that goes on in Africa, even in the face of hunger and famine.

If they still think that we all continue in the religion that we are born, they simply need to examine the history of Abrahamic religions. They were at the cross roads of conflicting ideas. This is where the east and the west ideologies clashed. The Israelites were constantly under the threat of being engulfed by neighbouring religions and beliefs. Yet the Abrahamic religions stood the test of time. Saint Paul himself went to the heart of philosophical debate, the marketplace of ideas and gods—the Greek Aeropagus—and preached Christianity and won over the whole of Europe and its barbaric paganism. We are not sure why the atheists are trying to reinvent the wheel here.

From the ethics perspective, the golden rule may have appeared in many religions and cultures, but it is always in a passive form: "don't do unto others what you don't want them to do to you." This is a call for inaction.

But only in Christianity, the golden rule calls for action: "Do unto others as you would want them to do to you." There is clear empirical evidence that Christians are the most charitable people anywhere in the world—even in India where many of them are relatively poor. To the extent that our charity is often misinterpreted as an attempt to subtly convert others to Christianity.

In a debate, Christopher Hitchens expressed his wonder as to why God chose to reveal Himself to the Israelite peasants rather than to Egyptians, Indians, or the Chinese whose civilizations were far greater at that time. But a basic knowledge of geography shows the revelation was brilliantly placed in space and time. We know Hitchens did not pay attention during his Sunday school classes, perhaps he did not pay attention even in his history and geography classes. The Middle East is at the cross roads of major civilizations of the East and West. Many great emperors would transverse that area in order to conquer other kingdoms. Jesus revealed Himself at the precise time when Rome had connections with all the major civilizations in the world. For the spreading of the gospel, no other time and place in history would have been more perfect than this.

There are others who ask as to why Jesus did not come at a time when there were video cameras around to record all His miracles and His resurrection. We would like to remind them that this is in the agenda. The prophecy mentioned in Revelation 1:7 clearly predicts His return in the age of video cameras and televisions through which all mankind will behold Him. At which point, every knee shall bow and every tongue confess His name. (Rom 14:11.)

Key Summary

As honest seekers of truth we should eliminate all those religions that are based on myths. By doing that, we eliminate almost all of them, barring a handful. Among the historical ones found in the world only the ethical monotheistic religions stand apart from the others. It is a form of exclusive monotheism in which God is the source for one standard of morality and who guides humanity through ethical principles.

Even among the ethical monotheistic ones, only in Christianity is there a zeal for truth and tolerance of falsity (without resorting to violence or judgement.) With its unique concepts of the unity of humanity, together with forgiveness and forbearance, Christianity becomes the most practical and livable religion on the planet.

While all the religions of the world are sincere quests of man trying to understand the mind of God, the Abrahamic religions are revelations of God given to mankind. Christ being the fullest revelation of God.

WHY CHRISTIANITY IS UNIQUE

A religion cannot profess to be propagating truth when its foundations are mythical, no matter how profound the philosophical insights found in them. As mentioned before, if we remove all religions that are founded on myths, only a few handful of contenders will be left. And among the historical ones, a strong case can be made for ethical monotheism.

We have already seen that all the three Abrahamic religions are historical and ethical monotheistic. Ironically, Jesus Christ is mentioned in scriptures of all the three of them. In the Old Testament which Jews follow, there are prophecies of a prophet to come in the end times which Christians believe would be Jesus in His second coming (in fact, the messianic Jews already believe in Jesus.) And in the Quran, Jesus is already venerated as a prophet who will return. If there ever is a single person who has the potential to unite all the three Abrahamic faiths then it is none other than Jesus Christ himself.

Of the historical ones, we find only Jesus claiming divinity, unlike Buddha who did not even confirm whether God exists or not. Jesus did not say "This is the way" but said "I am the Way." Jesus did not say "This is the truth" but said "I am the Truth." He also claimed a unique relationship with God. We have strong reasons to believe that the birth, life, death, and resurrection of Jesus Christ is unprecedented in history. The atheists or people of other religions may not agree with this, but what they cannot disagree with is the fact that no other individual in the history of humanity has transformed so many individuals, nations, and entire civilizations on this planet and made it a more humane place to live in. This is a brute historical fact.

Unlike conventional historic records, the Bible is unique. Usually it is the king who orders that records be made of his heroic achievements and usually the winner of wars gets to write a skewed history. Not so in the case of Biblical authors. Kings are often, if not always, condemned by the prophets for not following the commandments of God. Not only their successes but their utter failings are recorded with meticulous detail. And it does not stop with pointing out the flaws of kings, but also of the prophets and priests that lived in those times.

In archaeology, many have learned the hard way that absence of evidence is not evidence of absence. Although there is extra-Biblical evidence for nearly fifty-three persons mentioned in the Old Testament, many sceptics did not believe that King David could have existed. That was until Tel Dan Stele was discovered. This inscription dating to 870-750 BCE is the earliest non-Biblical mention of the House of David.

Of the fifty-three persons mentioned in the Old Testament who have extra-Biblical evidence of their existence, fourteen of these are kings of Israel and Judah mentioned in the two books of Kings. New circumstantial evidence is emerging on complexes built by David in Khirbet Qeiyafa and defensive walls built by Solomon in Jerusalem. Even the pools of Siloam (where Jesus healed the blind man) and Bethesda have been unearthed in Jerusalem.

No credible historian can deny the historicity of Jesus. Even atheists like Bart Ehrman (one of the most knowledgeable New Testament scholars and academic historians today) have no doubt that Jesus was a historical person. In his book *Did Jesus Exist?* Bart Ehrman methodically demolishes the "mythicist" arguments by marshalling evidence from the Bible and the wider historical record of the ancient world.

The best source of evidence are eyewitnesses. Even judges and historians always rely on eyewitnesses. The authors of the synoptic gospels had gathered data from such eyewitnesses (I Corinthians 15:6.) There may be minor differences in chronology and circumstances within the synoptic gospels but none of them affect the central doctrines of Christianity and what Jesus said about Himself. We must remember that these gospels were written in separate places by different people and yet there is remarkable agreement between them. This itself should attest to the reliability of the information found in the gospels.

Even scepticism needs to be rationalized. If there was only one eyewitness who was drunk, then we have reasons to be sceptical. But if there were multiple sober witnesses then we have no rational reason to doubt. And if the witness himself was a sceptic like Saint Paul then there is absolutely no reason to doubt. The problem with most of the sceptics is when the gospels agree verbatim, they assume it was copied from another common source even while having no evidence to present for such an assumption. Why not interpret the similarity by assuming multiple sources that witnessed an authentic common event?

We should also remember that the early Christians were anything but blind believers, although there were disagreements between them on which books were authentic yet all of them ratified the gospels we currently find in the New Testament. While the synoptic gospels give facts and figures, the Gospel of Saint John gives the most accurate theological interpretation of what happened in history. We have reasons to believe that the source of information for this gospel was the youngest disciple of Jesus (and the last to die) who had a remarkable "near-death experience" in the spirit on the island of Patmos. Soon after which he went on to record his experiences in the Book of Revelation. Reason why his gospel has the clearest vision of the divinity of Christ. "I am the light of this world" takes a profound new meaning in context of the research done on NDEs.

Josephus was a Jewish historian who lived closest to the time of Jesus. He records most of the historical figures that are mentioned in the New Testament including Herod, Pilate, Caiaphas the High Priest, John the Baptist, and even James the brother of our Lord. He also mentions Jesus twice (Antiquities of the Jews–Book XVIII 64 and XX 200) but scholars think one of the mentions may have been changed. But the debate is how much was altered and not the mention itself.

If that is not enough, twenty-three people (mainly political figures) mentioned in the New Testament have extra-Biblical evidence that they have indeed existed at the time of Christ. There is also strong circumstantial evidence that we have discovered the house of Peter (which was later converted into a place of worship in Capernaum) and the childhood home of Jesus in Nazareth, or one which the earliest Christians believed when they built a Byzantine church on it. The sources for all the evidence presented in this chapter can be found in the Biblical Archaeology Review website—*www.biblicalarchaeology.org.*

No other ancient religion has such archaeological evidence to support its authenticity. Since they cannot ignore such important archaeological evidence, the atheists now change their strategy and claim that the Bible is historical fiction. They admit that people and places mentioned in the Bible are true, but now demand evidence of the narrative itself, which kind of reeks of double standards (see next two paras below.) We are not sure how much more evidence is needed to convince them. Do they expect us to go back in time and get a video recording of all the events mentioned in the Bible? Jesus was right about not bothering to present any more evidence to such eternal pessimists, "…neither will they be persuaded, though one rose from the dead." (Luke 16:31.)

Dan Barker is actually fulfilling the above prophecy when he says that even if it were proven that Jesus rose from the dead, it would still not mean that He is the Son of God. Well, in that case even the fossils don't prove evolution. They are just bones of dead animals. Such extreme scepticism of the militant atheists can even relapse into solipsism—we could even be nothing but a brain in a vat. We cannot even begin to do our science with confidence under such circumstances. There is plenty of convergent evidence in the Gospels that Christ claimed to be divine and was crucified for it.

Recorded history of the Gospels has much more probability of being true than speculations of pre-history like abiogenesis. As pointed out in the chapter on evolution, we still have no clue how life itself arose. We have no clue if natural selection is enough to account for the major transitions of life and all its complexity. The origin of species is trivial compared to the problem of the origin of phyla seen during the Cambrian explosion. Yet the atheists have blind faith that all of the above do not need intelligent causation. How do they know that?

Most atheists think we should not trust the Gospels because they were written by believers decades later. But that is putting the cart before the horse. How did they come to be believers in the first place? Even before the Gospels were written, Christianity spread like wild fire in the Mediterranean region. On the flip side, if we apply the same logic to the books on evolution, we should be dumping all of those in the dustbin too, since they are all written by believers in evolution millions of years after the events are supposed to have taken place.

Even today, every event is reported in different ways and perspectives by different newspapers. Similar is the case with the four Gospels. There may be chronological and other differences between them, but all the four Gospels agree on all the central doctrines of Christianity. The usual atheistic excuse is that these records were made decades later, forgetting that the disciples of Jesus lived for decades after His life, death, and resurrection. We also know that the information in the synoptic Gospels came from Hebrew and Aramaic speaking sources—the very languages that Jesus spoke. Those sources also knew the geography of Galilee and Jerusalem well enough to detail it in the Gospels.

For a moment, even if we disregard the Gospels and look at the earliest of the New Testament documents—which is the First book of Thessalonians—we find all the central doctrines and claims of Christianity in it. Ironically, this book has been authored by Saint Paul, who was once vehemently against Christianity. For further reading, we recommend *Jesus and the Eyewitnesses* by New Testament scholar Richard Bauckham. He builds a strong case for the authenticity of the Gospels—that they are based on the testimony of those who personally knew Jesus.

Historians generally agree that the baptism of Jesus, the appointing of disciples, His criticism of the Levitical priesthood, and His subsequent crucifixion by the Romans have indeed taken place in history. They have increasing difficulty in separating the ministry of Jesus with the miracles He performed, which shows that miracles were integral to His ministry. To this general consensus, we would like to add the resurrection. We know from historical records that the early Christians were expecting Jesus to return any moment during their lives to the extent that they sold everything they had and donated it to the Church and lived as a community. If Jesus was dead and his bones were still around, who were they expecting to return? If Saul wanted to bust Christianity, he just needed to show them the tomb of Jesus with His bones in it. Instead, we have the testimony of the resurrection from Christianity's enemy number one. What more evidence can we ask for, than the testimony of one who was against Christianity itself?

Notice how the atheists ask for meticulous evidence of everything that Jesus did and at the same time allow dollops of ambiguity when it comes to the hypothesis of evolution. We have already pointed out that evolution is a messy amalgam of assumptions, assertions, and speculations. It is easily the most over-speculated theory in the history of science.

In contrast, Christianity is easily the most scrutinized and the most researched religion in the world. More books have been written on Christianity than about any other religion or subject in the world. The Holy Bible is the most read and the most translated book in the world. Friedrich Nietzsche thought that they would have no use of the Bible in the future. Ironically, it is his philosophy that has been sent to the scrap heap of history. All this testifies the enduring value of Christianity and its relevance even in this scientific age.

The atheists are not only bad in science and rationality but also in interpreting history. In his book *The New Atheist Denial of History*, Borden W. Painter clearly shows how the atheists have distorted history. He points out the lack of historical credibility in their claims when compared to the conventional criteria used by mainstream historians.

The rapid spread of Christianity is itself unique in history. No other religion spread so rapidly and widely as Christianity, and that too in the face of tremendous persecution. Even before any of the books of the New Testament were written, Christianity spread like wild fire throughout the Mediterranean region in spite of persecution by the mighty Roman Empire. Saint Paul rightly observes that they came to believe not by empty words but by the power of God manifest in those days.

Gamaliel who lived during Jesus' time had this advice for the Pharisees and Scribes who did not believe in Jesus: "...Ye men of Israel, take heed to yourselves what ye intend to do as touching these men. For before these days rose up Theudas, boasting himself to be somebody; to whom a number of men, about four hundred, joined themselves: who was slain; and all, as many as obeyed him, were scattered, and brought to nought. After this man rose up Judas of Galilee in the days of the taxing, and drew away much people after him: he also perished; and all, even as many as obeyed him, were dispersed. And now I say unto you, Refrain from these men, and let them alone: for if this counsel or this work be of men, it will come to nought: But if it be of God, ye cannot overthrow it; lest haply ye be found even to fight against God." (Acts 5:35-39.) How true are these words and if Gamaliel lived in these days, he would (like Apostle Thomas) have knelt and professed the divinity of Christ.

All the above evidence for Christianity demands a verdict. Where did this great zeal for spreading the Gospel come from even after their prophet was presumed dead? What did the Apostles and their families risk all their lives for? Why did they take great pains to travel throughout the Roman world as far as India to spread the Gospel? Why did the early Christians scoff at persecutions and willingly die for Christ? Why were they not afraid of the mighty Roman Emperor? These are hard questions every atheist has to answer. Or perhaps they can heed to the wise words of Gamaliel mentioned earlier, "…if it be a work of God, ye cannot overthrow it."

Like any scientific theory, Christianity also makes certain predictions on how the world will be at the second coming of Christ. Ironically, it describes the current world exactly as it is. The following should be obvious to anyone who has cared to look around or read the newspaper headlines: "For men shall be lovers of their own selves, covetous, boasters, proud, blasphemers, disobedient to parents, unthankful, unholy…" (2 Timothy 3:2) and "Nation shall rise against nation, and kingdom against kingdom:" (Luke 21:10.) Perhaps even militant atheism was predicted by Jesus: "…Nevertheless when the Son of man cometh, shall He find faith on the earth?" (Luke 18:8.)

If we further correlate what the Holy Bible is saying regarding humanity and existence in general, it is exactly what one might expect if Bible were true. A brilliant creation gone awry by the disobedience of man. A great gulf of space and time (since time is also a dimension according to Einstein) separates humanity from God. Without God's presence, the fallen creation is mean, brutal, and evil by nature. But there is also hope, a dispensation of grace has been given for humanity to repent.

Anyone who surveys the various religions of the world with an impartial mind will be struck by the simplicity of the Christian message. To receive salvation, one does not need any secret knowledge or chant a unique mantra. Realize your evil nature, confess your true state, repent, and accept the gospel of Jesus Christ—it is mission accomplished.

Christianity is also unique in giving humanity a greater role than any other beings on earth unlike Hinduism and Jainism wherein one could be reborn in the plant or animal kingdom. In India, the cow is venerated and is more important than humans. In fact, one could even be lynched for eating cow meat. Only in Christianity is mankind given dominion of the planet and if that is not enough, they are also promised to be co-heirs with Jesus Christ in His kingdom to come. No other religion has such a glorious vision for mankind. The God of Christianity is no celestial despot as Hitchens and Krauss envisage. If only both of them paid a little more attention to their Sunday school lessons, they would not have come up with such an absurd view of God.

All the evidence presented in this chapter should convince even hardest of sceptics that Christianity is easily the most historical, rationally consistent, humanistic, and livable religion on the planet. If Humanist organizations seek to be rationally consistent, they should defenestrate the atheists and the scientific materialists, and welcome the Christian Apologists into their fold instead.

Key Summary

A religion cannot profess to be propagating truth when its foundations are mythical, no matter how profound the philosophical insights found in them. As mentioned before, if we remove all religions that are founded on myths, only a few handful of contenders will be left. And among the historical ones, a strong case can be made for ethical monotheism.

Of the historical ones, we find only Jesus claiming divinity, unlike Buddha who did not even confirm if God exists or not. Jesus did not say "This is the way" but said "I am the Way." Jesus did not say "This is the truth" but said "I am the Truth." He also claimed a unique relationship with God. We have strong reasons to believe that the birth, life, death, and resurrection of Jesus Christ is unprecedented in history. The atheists or people of other religions may not agree with this but what they cannot disagree with is the fact that no other individual in the history of humanity has transformed so many individuals, nations, and entire civilizations on this planet and made it a more humane place to live in. This is a brute historical fact.

Historians generally agree that the baptism of Jesus, the appointing of disciples, His criticism of the Levitical priesthood, and His crucifixion by the Romans have indeed taken place in history. They have increasing difficulty in separating the ministry of Jesus with the miracles He performed, which shows that miracles were integral to His ministry. To this general consensus, we would like to add the resurrection. We know from historical records that the early Christians were expecting Jesus to return any moment during their lives to the extent that they sold everything they had and donated it to the Church and lived as a community. If Jesus was dead and his bones were still around, who were they expecting to return? If Saul wanted to bust Christianity, he just needed to show them the tomb of Jesus with His bones in it. Instead, we have the testimony of the resurrection from Christianity's enemy number one. What more evidence can we ask for, than the testimony of one who was against Christianity itself?

No other ancient religion has such archaeological evidence to support its authenticity. Since they cannot ignore such important archaeological evidence, the atheists now change their strategy and claim that the Bible is historical fiction. They admit that people and places mentioned in the Bible are true, but now demand evidence of the narrative itself, which kind of reeks of double standards in context of the origin of the universe and life. We are not sure how much more evidence is needed to convince them. Do they expect us to go back in time and get a video recording of all the events mentioned in the Bible? Jesus was right about not bothering to present any more evidence to such eternal pessimists, "…neither will they be persuaded, though one rose from the dead." (Luke 16:31.)

All the evidence presented in this chapter should convince even hardest of sceptics that Christianity is easily the most historical, rationally consistent, humanistic, and livable religion on the planet. If Humanist organizations seek to be rationally consistent, they should defenestrate the atheists and the scientific materialists, and welcome the Christian Apologists into their fold instead.

Scripture versus science

Nowhere are the atheistic arguments more ridiculous than when they quote scripture out of context and criticize it. It is baffling to see atheists time and again trivialize the scriptures on whim and without setting the proper context or the necessary ground rules.

The Holy Bible is not a book of physics, chemistry, or biology. I am not sure how the atheists miss that. Instead, it is looking at history and civics from a theological perspective. Flip a few pages and you will see that the Old Testament is also the history of the nation of Israel, and the New Testament is the history of Jesus Christ and his commissioning of the apostles to spread the good news. The civics part is the sermon on the mount which has unambiguous instructions on how to live our lives. Only fools would look for details about the spin of an electron in religious scriptures and greater fools look for details about the golden rule, "Do unto others as you would want them to do unto you," in a textbook of atomic physics. But this is exactly what atheists like Richard Dawkins and Sam Harris are attempting to do. They read biology when they should be reading theology and read theology when they should be reading biology. They ask theological questions and expect scientific answers and ask scientific questions on theological constructs found in the Bible.

Among the various creation narratives of great civilizations—like the Greeks, the Babylonians, the Egyptians, and the Indians—the Biblical narrative was light years ahead of its time and is closest to what science is currently revealing. Isaac Asimov was right when he said in his book *In the beginning* that "There is no version of primeval history, preceding the discoveries of modern science, that is as rational and as inspiring as that of the book of Genesis." Even Peter Atkins in his book *On Being* admits that the Biblical narrative is much calmer and mature than other creation accounts.

We now know that the universe had a definitive beginning and was not eternal as Aristotle envisaged, the diversity of life was created at different stages, and man was the last to come. Homo became Sapiens (wise) on the day he understood that his Creator must necessarily exist and began to call upon His name (Gen 4:26.) Unfortunately, many these days are becoming atavistic and are randomly mutating back to Homo Stupidus!

The creation versus evolution debate is therefore fundamentally flawed because one is talking about the origins while the other is talking about the process. The Genesis account makes no claims of describing the process except that the process needs to include intelligence, while evolution has no clue about the origins of our cosmos and life, and conveniently takes them both for granted. Both can be complimentary to each other when both make a provision for intelligent causation. Unfortunately, it is the belligerence of the scientific materialists and their insistence on blind chance (which is both unscientific and irrational) that is creating a rift when there is none.

Anyone out there still arguing whether it took six days or billions of years for the creation of this universe and life are outdated in their physics by a century, or do not seem to have a full understanding of the theory of relativity. We now know that it is pointless to talk about absolute time. According to the theory of relativity, space and time are intertwined. We cannot separate one from the other and according to the Bible, a great gulf separates humanity from God (Luke 16:26) who is the first cause and the source of all creation.

But if the atheists still insist on seeing scientific truths in the Holy Bible, we want to know science of which age do they want to see in the scriptures? If they want it to represent current science as we know it today, then there would have been atheists in the past ridiculing concepts of relativity and quantum physics until the time of their discovery. Suppose the scriptures said that time is relative, it would have earned ridicule right from the Greeks until the time of Einstein. Not to mention how gleeful the atheists of those times would have been if the Bible said that the earth was a round sphere. Every atheist in history would have had a field day ridiculing believers by asking why people living at the bottom of the sphere do not fall off. If the Bible had mentioned sciences as we currently know it now, then everyone in history would have to accept it based on blind faith until the time of those discoveries. If the atheists want to see the ultimate truth in the Bible, then maybe the after-life and the kingdom of God mentioned therein are exactly that!

On the flip side, even if they want to see current science in the Bible, how do they know that current science is the most accurate representation of reality? Albert Michelson thought we were done with the fundamental sciences in 1894 itself. The theory of relativity and quantum physics in the early 1900s turned everything upside down later. Simon Newcomb thought in 1888 that there was very little left in the heavens to be discovered, yet the Hubble space telescope continues to alter our perspective even today. Currently, physicists are struggling to reconcile quantum theory with theory of relativity and who knows how that will change our perspective? We all know that a single experiment can wreak havoc to a theory that is currently accepted. It is for good reason that the Holy Bible keeps science out. It deals with eternal truths and not ephemeral ones.

Science itself, with its half knowledge, misled humanity many times during its two-and-a-half millennia of existence since Thales of Miletus. Ptolemy misled humanity by mathematically formalizing the earth-centered view of our solar system (which Aristotle had envisaged) with sad consequences. Even the greatest mind of his day, Aristotle misled the world by postulating an eternal universe while current research shows that it had a beginning. The Holy Bible does remarkably well to be silent about scientific theories which are constantly changing and refining.

We would also like to remind the atheists that the Holy Bible began to be written three millennia back. It is disingenuous and anachronistic of them to compare it with modern-day science textbooks. In the Bronze Age, astronomy was called astrology, and doctors were called shamans, while chemistry was called alchemy just a few centuries ago. Is anyone ridiculing science looking at its past? That would be absurd. When the Bible is set in its time, it was light years ahead of others—including the Greeks—in its creation narrative, its conception of God, and of governance. Israel had a constitution—The Torah—centuries before the Greeks could think of governance. It applied to the common man as well as to the kings and the priests, no one was above the law unlike in Rome where the king was elevated to the status of God. The Old Testament was a shadow of what was to be revealed by Jesus Christ and currently the New Testament is our rule book.

Even though the Old Testament was written three millennia back, the first few chapters of Genesis do have a valuable insight for humanity today. Seek character and compassion before you eat the fruit of knowledge. If God had indeed revealed the true nature of physical reality to the fallen man, then humanity would have self-destructed long before Christ was born. Knowledge is power and before we have power in our hands, we must ensure we have our ethical framework and governance in place. And that is exactly what the Bible focuses on. Imagine the pandemonium if the peasants of Bronze Age were empowered with accurate information about atomic physics and chemistry, they would have blown themselves to extinction. The Bible had its priorities right by not revealing the true nature of physical reality to mankind before giving them an ethical framework first. It would have been like placing a dynamite in the hands of an infant.

Another reason why God may not have revealed the true nature of reality to mankind was their dim understanding at that time. If God had uttered any equation of physics, it would have left Abraham scratching his head until his death. How could he comprehend the astonishing scale of numbers that current science reveals, when he was unable to count beyond his sheep and

166

oxen? We start teaching every child elementary truths before going deeper. That was probably what the Bible set out to do for civilizations that were still in their infancy.

While it is obvious to every Christian, the atheists somehow miss the crucial point that the Bible is primarily concerned with the salvation of man and everything else is secondary. It has an urgent message for humanity on how they can return to God. If someone were walking down a street unaware of a car approaching him at top speed, it would be futile to preach Newtonian physics to him at that point of time. We would rather shout and warn him to get out of the way. This is exactly what the Bible is doing for humanity. It is not here to teach science, but rather calling on humanity to return to God.

What then is the relationship between science and scripture? While science is a puerile commentary of nature; scripture and religion set the agenda for the future. For a penny of comfort, science has given us a pound of disaster. Religion can very well do without it. But science without religion and its moral compass spells disaster for humanity.

Since science is an endeavour of man, it constantly changes, but scripture does not. Many view this as a disadvantage but we don't think so. As pointed out earlier, it would be very dangerous to open up religion for revision. That will be a slippery slope from which humanity can never recover. Democracies, politicians, philosophers, and scientists will do well to keep their hands off the morals and ethics specified in the New Testament. Stalin and Mao went that way with disastrous consequences.

Atheists always dwell in the past and whine continually about wrongs committed by the church in history. They conveniently cherry-pick from two millennia of Christianity's history and forget what atheism has done in the few decades of its existence in Russia and China. What guarantee can they give that history will not repeat itself? What empirical evidence can they give that atheism will be a force for good? Can they even define what is good in the first place?

Of course, there may be problematic passages in the Bible, but science has its own set of problematic equations. It has been more than a century since the quantum and relativity theories were postulated, yet science has been unable to reconcile them. And in biology we have the origin of life and sudden development of phyla in the Cambrian period. The biologists have no clue how these could have happened. Why then pick the Bible while letting science go scot free? If they blindly believe that science will resolve this in the future then maybe the Biblical problems will also be resolved when we have the fullest revelation of Christ when He returns.

Key Summary

Nowhere are the atheistic arguments more ridiculous than when they quote the scripture out of context and criticize it. It is baffling to see the atheists time and again trivialize the scriptures on whim and without setting the proper context or the necessary ground rules.

The Holy Bible is not a book of physics, chemistry, or biology. I am not sure how the atheists miss that. Instead, it is looking at history and civics from a theological perspective. Flip a few pages and you will see that the Old Testament is the history of the nation of Israel, and the New Testament is the history of Jesus Christ and his commissioning of the apostles to spread the good news. The civics part is the sermon on the mount which has unambiguous instructions on how to live our lives. Only fools would look for details about the spin of an electron in religious scriptures and greater fools look for details about the golden rule, "Do unto others as you would want them to do unto you," in a textbook of atomic physics.

What then is the relationship between science and scripture? While science is a puerile commentary of nature; scripture and religion set the agenda for the future. For a penny of comfort, science has given us a pound of disaster. Religion can very well do without it. But science without religion and its moral compass spells disaster for mankind.

INTELLECTUAL INCOHERENCE OF ATHEISM

Many atheists usually point out to the diverse religions found in the world and the various denominations within Christianity and claim that theism cannot be coherently justified. But is their atheistic worldview any more coherent? This chapter will blow that myth to smithereens. When we examine militant atheism more closely, it is much more self-contradictory and incoherent than theism. We will begin by showing the general incoherence within their worldview and then go on to show how atheists themselves have contradictory or conflicting viewpoints on many things. You might find this chapter a bit repetitive but it is needed to see the incoherence of atheism.

Most atheists keep trivializing and demeaning humanity. Stephen Hawking thinks we are chemical scum, Sam Harris thinks we are the stuff that yeasts are made of, Daniel Dennett thinks we are some kind of zombies who hallucinate consciousness while Dawkins claims that we are lumbering robots built by our genes for survival rather than rational thought. How is it then, that such chemical scum is making grandiose statements about the non-existence of God and writing books like *The End of Faith* and *The God Delusion?*

If we are indeed what the atheists say we are, I would dump all scientific knowledge and rational enquiry into the dustbin counting them as subjective and parochial nonsense. Atheists cannot even begin to do their science with confidence in such a worldview. Given that current science has no clue on how our brain functions or how consciousness itself arises. They are the ones who should be most sceptical about their rational deductions than anyone else. If atheism is right then atheism is wrong.

Contrast that with the theistic worldview. We are made in the image of God, we have free will to do objective science and our brain has been designed by an intelligent Creator to introspect and seek truth. Science and rational inquiry in such a worldview makes much more sense than in an atheistic worldview. Theism is thus reinforcing, while atheism is self-defeating.

Perhaps one of the greatest misconceptions that most atheists have is that if science explains something then there is no need of God. We have already pointed out that this is an utterly fallacious assumption. Science does not make God redundant in the same way Ford cannot be made redundant even if we can explain how an automobile engine works. This is a *non sequitur.*

Even if science can answer all the difficult questions in the future, how do they know that the answers which science finds will still support their atheistic worldview? Unless of course, they claim to be some kind of soothsayers of scientism. How do they know that the ultimate nature of reality will never point to God? Atheism is not only unscientific and irrational but also against the very spirit of scientific enquiry.

Claiming that there is no evidence for the existence of God while having incomplete knowledge is inadmissible in the legal courts. Instead, they will be admonished for being lazy. If evidence presented by the theists is not convincing, they still cannot appeal to "lack of evidence" an excuse. They should instead confess that "they don't know" and admit their ignorance. This is an agnostic position and not an atheistic one.

On the flip side, one can be a theist with half knowledge. One intelligent radio signal from outer space is enough to prove the existence of extra-terrestrial intelligence. The evidence of intelligent causation given in the previous chapters and the power, order, and wisdom found in nature are enough for us to believe in a powerful and wise Creator God. Theism therefore can be rationalized even with half knowledge.

In the chapter on evolution, we have seen how it cannot be a scientific theory since it is founded on "randomness" which has no room in science. In fact, it is antithetical to the method of science that is trying to comprehend order found in nature. Science has no clue how life originated while the evolutionists conveniently assume its existence. No other theory in science assumes the very thing it sets out to explain. Evolution is therefore much ado about nothing. If we take away these twin crutches of militant atheism— science and evolution—it becomes a lame worldview.

They claim science is fact-based while religion is faith-based, which is utter flapdoodle. Science is as much faith and revelation based as religion. Unless the phenomenon reveals itself to us, we will have no clue about it. Dark matter and energy are grim reminders of that. We have no clue about ninety-five percent of the universe because nature has not yet revealed that to us yet.

We currently have no clue how our own brain functions. Is it not blind faith that we accept the output of a processor that we don't understand? The very epistemological foundations of science are faith-based. Many reductionists think that consciousness is a pointless emergent phenomena of the brain. In that case, all scientific theories are "revelations" of the brain to the conscious mind. How can they trust such revelations when there can be no free will in their worldview? Even the experiments conducted in the neural sciences depend upon revelations of their subjects' experiences. Why not dump all neural sciences as well?

The atheists have blind faith on the homilies of Saint Richard and their holy writ called "On the origin of species" even when many things written in it have been falsified. Even when it does not answer questions regarding the origin of life and of phyla—the fundamental body plans of all life—which are more fundamental than speciation. How does Dawkins know that natural selection alone is enough for all the major transitions of life, except by blind faith? What demonstrable evidence can he give that natural selection alone was enough for the transitions from prokaryotes to eukaryotes, from unicellular to multicellular, from asexual to sexual reproduction, from simple divisions to complex morphogenesis, and the creation of all phyla during the Cambrian explosion? Making blanket statements like "evolution is enough" is neither scientific nor rational. Instead, they are atheistic assertions made out of blind faith which science will not vouch for. There is no way we can demonstrate or verify such grandiose statements empirically.

Are the atheists not placing blind faith on the homilies of Saint Lawrence when he preaches that a universe can pop out of absolutely nothing when the only evidence he can present is a non-peer-reviewed popular paperback? We know that science is merely discovering how the universe works and not inventing it. Are his equations some abracadabra spells that could magically exist in absolute nothingness, appear suddenly on its own without any causation and conjure up the spatial dimensions, time, energy, and the laws of physics that govern them—all in an instant?

Are the atheists not blindly hoping in the highly speculative theories like the string theory and parallel universes even when they don't have a shred of empirical evidence? Many are willing to believe them just to dodge the brute fact of fine-tuning. Merely pointing to a mathematical framework does not guarantee that string theory represents reality. Even the Ptolemaic equations used to have a consistent mathematical framework (with minor aberrations,) but we now know how utterly false the system turned out to be.

They blindly believe that the earth came to be in the Goldilocks zone by cosmic luck and that life arose out of a fortuitous concourse of atoms. They believe random mutations are responsible for the wonderful innovations and complexity of life. They think consciousness is a chance emergent phenomenon of the brain. All these are atheistic and materialistic assertions that can neither be tested nor demonstrated. As pointed out earlier, "random" and "chance" are mere English words devoid of any meaning in science.

Ironically, it is the theists who are presenting brute facts of science and empirical evidence: the origin of the universe and of life, fine-tuning of the universe, the intricate structure of living cells, the complex process of morphogenesis, and the complexity of the brain. While the atheists are making up speculative myths that the universe came out of absolute nothing and all the complexity found in nature is sheer dumb luck—neither of which is scientific or rational. Appealing to "nothing" and "chance" is to abandon science.

In almost all cases it is turning out that the atheists are having more blind faith than the theists, which they conveniently term "confidence." If the scientists had enough faith in the standard model to build the LHC to detect Higgs, why are we not allowed to have faith in our standard model—Christianity—and that we will detect the spiritual dimension one day when we die?

Nowhere is the incoherence within atheism more evident than in their diverse views on free will. Sam Harris denies free will completely. Daniel Dennett invents an oxymoron "deterministic free will" to postulate a vague notion of free will. Their spat on this topic have already embarrassed the atheistic community. Michael Shermer points to a few unproven speculations in his book *The Moral Arc* to say that we may have some kind of free will, knowing that science cannot vouch for unproven speculations. Richard Dawkins cleverly says he is undecided on the subject knowing fully well that he will be in a fix if he says he has free will (a strict no-no in a reductionist worldview) and he will be in a greater fix if he professes that he has no free will (since science will cease to be objective.) As pointed out earlier, free will is impossible in their reductionist view since they assert that our mind is nothing but our materialistic brain. And in a world without free will there can be no objective science or morals. Many atheists reject a belief in a theistic God but conveniently assume that they are some theistic demigods who have transcended nature to have free will to do objective science.

When we closely examined the principle objections of the atheists in the previous chapters, we found that those objections are neither rational nor scientific. There is incoherence even in the objections they raise. Some atheists think that philosophy is useless, but go on to use lame philosophical excuses like celestial teapots, god-of-the-gaps, and the problem of evil to justify their unbelief. While a few others talk about ethics, which is a branch of philosophy. Few others assert metaphysical naturalism which is a philosophical presupposition, even when there is scientific evidence to the contrary. They ridicule theology but bring up theodicy. They also think the "why" questions are pointless, but then go on to disbelieve precisely because of questions like "why is there suffering in the world?"

Jerry Coyne says science has nothing to do with morality while Sam Harris and Michael Shermer claim science can determine human values. They claim that they can be good, even when atheism is amoral and has no definition of what is good. Sam Harris claims that we cannot have free will and then goes on to blame, ridicule, and condemn religious people. It is disingenuous of the atheists to write books and take up debates without first resolving this fundamental paradox of free will in their worldview.

They criticize various religious moral frameworks without having any basis for judging the same. It is like someone appealing to justice in a country which has no constitution to base its judgements on. They nitpick on three millennia of religious wrong-doing while conveniently forget that the atheistic regimes of China and Russia have done more harm to humanity in a few decades than religion has done in the past three thousand years.

Atheists are amoral—they have no code of conduct to base their moral judgements on—and as a result they could be cynic, nihilist, epicurean, or even be whimsical and moody. There are bound to be as many denominations in atheism as there are atheists because they have no common moral thread to weave them together. The militant atheists conveniently assume humanism even when their worldview contradicts it. Humanism, like science needs

Christian foundations to make sense. Humanism minus Christianity equals to puerile speciesism. Historically, atheists have been moral relativists but seem to have randomly mutated to moral realists. In reality, their worldview logically leads to cynicism, nihilism, and even extreme skepticism. There is nothing within atheism to sort one from the other. We are sure that many atheists would not agree with their fellow humanists regarding prostitution, incest, and drugs. It is shocking to note that few atheists see nothing wrong with them.

They advocate secularism and say that religion should be kept out of governance and criticize Christianity for not condemning slavery which was an official state practice during Roman times. Like the southerners in United States, they believe that the Bible justifies slavery even when there are clear ordinances in the Old Testament itself to set them free. But the real paradox is while they condemn slavery on one hand, they call us lumbering robots and slaves without free will on the other. How liberating is that? What freedom, liberty, and justice can we expect from such a worldview?

Atheists have various "scientific" explanations for belief, some base it on the "God" gene, some on evolutionary adaptations (cognitive by-product theory), and some on the way our brain works, which they say is attuned for pattern recognition. But how come atheism is beyond such naturalistic explanations? Are they some mutants who have transcended nature and evolution? Who knows, there may be evolutionary reasons for their unbelief as well. Maybe they are rejecting Christianity because they can spread their genes without the restrictions of monogamy!

They also trace belief and behaviour to chemicals in the brain, yet somehow consider themselves transcendent mutants who have arisen above the biology and chemistry of their brains. As pointed out earlier, if they think I believe because I have excess of "theistocin" in my brain then maybe it is the deficiency of the same that makes one an atheist. Or maybe they possess an excess of another chemical called "atheistoxin." Where is the objectivity in science here?

Many atheists think mankind began to believe in God out of fear, but that does not preclude the objective existence of the phenomenon in question. It could be that a person began to believe in gravity when an apple plonked on his head or when he broke a bone by falling from a tree. But none of these have anything to do with the objective reality of gravity. Ditto regarding our belief in God. God as a first cause or an eternal source is a rational deduction beyond such petty speculations on how mankind came to believe.

They doubt the New Testament because it has been written decades later, but then go on to believe in abiogenesis which is supposed to have happened magically four billion years ago for which they have zero evidence. Most atheists agree that Jesus is a historical person while the mythicists bizarrely go against the consensus of historians. They ridicule the virgin birth even though it has been empirically observed in nature in some species of fishes, while they believe shaking and stirring of chemicals in a test tube and zapping it with electricity can create life. They ridicule resurrection while they themselves resurrect a robot and say it might be conscious some day when it reaches a certain complexity. They are sceptical of the recorded history of the Old Testament but blithely trust the frugal and fragmented fossil record, even when it contradicts gradual evolution and supports punctuated equilibrium.

They say that preaching of the cross is child abuse and go on to call that innocent child a genetically modified ape, a lumbering robot made of chemical scum that can have no free will. They go beyond what science and rationality can deduce and trouble the child by saying that life is pointless and the universe is without any purpose. They go on to teach her evolution as dogma, shooting down her innocent questions and heaping speculative "just-so" mythical stories on her innocent mind. They encourage her to burn all books which write against evolution. They impart scientific knowledge to the child even before teaching her ethics and empathy. They encourage her to go to the university and learn how to build atom bombs and discourage her from going to Sunday school where she would be taught never to use it.

They say science is open-ended and then go on to be utterly close-minded when it comes to the evidence presented for the existence of God and to evidence presented for intelligent causation. They setup huge radio telescopes to detect extra-terrestrial intelligence, but when we point to the fine-tuning of the universe which has infinitely more convincing evidence of intelligent causation than a puerile radio signal from outer space, they become holocaust deniers.

They ask us to question everything, except of course their holy writ called evolution. A recent study done by the Catholic University in Louvain, Belgium shows that it is the atheists that are less tolerant than the religious (Greg Wilford reports this in The Independent, dated 2 July 2017.) We don't actually need the above study, since we have experienced that first hand when we question evolution. If we question them on their close mindedness, they resort to smart talk. They tell us that they don't want to be so open minded that their brains fall off. But we think that those brains have already fallen off when they blindly accept that a universe popped out of absolutely nothing and that by zapping lightening into a chemical soup, bacteria can crawl out of their test tubes. There are many scientists who believe that natural selection is not enough to explain the complexity found in life. While the reductionists continue to assert that natural selection is enough, even in the face of contradicting evidence.

In some ways, the atheists are an epitome of dogmatism. They are not only close minded to the questions raised by the theists, but also dictate the sort of questions we should be asking. When Dawkins was asked what the purpose of life was, his reply was typical: "It's not a proper question to put, it doesn't deserve an answer."

They claim that the universe is pointless and then go on to advise us to make our own purpose, as if that will magically assume a great meaning. That life has no meaning and that the universe is pointless are grandiose atheistic assertions that true science will have nothing to do with. There is no scientific theory or rational deduction to validate these assertions. Atheistic scientists and rationalists have no business in making such irresponsible statements. In fact, as we have shown earlier, the development of the universe via the laws of physics and the development of life via a genetic code are exactly what you would expect to see in a teleological universe. They are physical manifestations of purposeful systems.

If God is deistic, they say He is callous. If God is theistic, they say He is petty. If God punishes wrong-doing, they say He is mean. If He is long suffering, they say He is impotent. And if He lays down His life for our sake, they reject him with indignation and self-righteousness. Dawkins asks why God couldn't just forgive mankind instead of dying on the cross while Christopher Hitchens wants justice meted out without mercy on criminals. By the way, if God had indeed "just" forgiven humanity then they would blame Him for being whimsical. If every denomination agrees on a doctrine, they call it dogmatic. If they don't agree then they are deemed to be incoherent. They judge God on moral issues without having any moral foundations of their own. Ironically, they are the ones who proclaim that we should accept phenomena as it is and not how we would whimsically like it to be. But then go on to reject God because He does not tickle their fancy. Does anyone reject gravity just because it caused suffering by plonking an apple on their head or that it is restraining them from floating freely like in fairy tales?

All such incoherence within atheism and the fundamental differences among them could easily be given different names and counted as different denominations within atheism. If there are so many differences among them in just two or three decades of their existence, imagine how many more denominations there will be in the next two millennia.

If they are trying to tell us that the only common thing that unites the atheists is their disbelief in God then the same applies to all the religions of the world. A belief in a Creator God is what unites all religions together. There is no difference between these two positions. Why then ask "which religion is true?" And then without waiting for a Christian response presume all of them to be wrong?

Key Summary

Many atheists usually point out to the diverse religions found in the world and the various denominations within Christianity and claim that theism cannot be coherently justified. But is their atheistic worldview any more coherent? When we examine militant atheism more closely, it is much more self-contradictory and incoherent than theism.

Atheists could be nihilists, sceptics, or cynics. They could even be communists or Maoists. Some believe in free will while others don't. Some think science can determine human values while others don't. Some are moral relativists while others believe in moral realism.

All such incoherence within atheism and the fundamental differences among them could easily be given different names and counted as different denominations within atheism. If there are so many differences among them in just two or three decades of their existence, imagine how many more denominations there will be in the next two millennia.

If they are trying to tell us that the only common thing that unites the atheists is their disbelief in God then the same applies to all the religions of the world. A belief in a Creator God is what unites all religions together. There is no difference between these two positions. Why then ask "which religion is true?" And then without waiting for a Christian response presume all of them to be wrong?

If I were in Oxford on that day

(This chapter is also an overview of the entire book and as such may seem repetitive. If you have read the previous chapters then you can skip to the end of the chapter where I have answered questions which the atheists have raised during the debate.)

"This house believes in God" was the proposition to be defended in the Oxford Union Debate on November 8, 2014. Here is what I would have said if I were invited...

I think, therefore I exist.

I exist, but I did not create myself.

Therefore, there exists an entity that created me.

You could point to my parents and say that they have created me, or you could point to a complex process like morphogenesis and attribute my existence to it. Although there is an element of truth in both these deductions and is useful to see the causal relationships, we think that they are ultimately petty, trivial, and myopic when one is trying to answer the deeper questions of existence. By pointing to the immediate preceding cause, we are merely passing the buck since one could then go on to ask who created my parents or how the process of morphogenesis come to be in the first place.

Suppose I set up a detailed contraption which at the press of a button in another country, triggers a remote-controlled gun to kill a certain deluded zoologist in Oxford. If you call in a typical atheist like Peter Atkins to be the judge, he would say "nothing but" the bullet had killed him. But if the investigators had some common sense, they will not buy such a trivial deduction and will probe deeper to trace the contraption to me—the first cause—and bring me to justice.

The first cause therefore is the root cause of my existence. Science now tells us that it takes incredible power in the form of energy, order in the form of laws and constants of physics, and wisdom of fine-tuning to make a universe which can then go on to create us. The first cause should therefore have all of these in place. Whatever science labels the first cause or the eternal source of all creation, we revere that entity as our Creator God. The only difference between science and religion then is in the nomenclature.

But where are the atheists going to get the incredible power, order, and wisdom found in our cosmos from? Unfortunately, science can never bail out atheism on the question of origins because of its causal methodology. Every effect must have a cause and this relapses into a *reduction ad absurdum ad infinitum.* "Ever learning, and never able to come to the knowledge of the truth." (2 Timothy 3:7.)

Funnily, the atheists believe that the universe popped out of absolutely nothing, that order is somehow inherent, and fine-tuning is sheer dumb luck. None of these assertions are scientific or rational. If they are telling us to abandon our intuitions about nature, including causality, then nature itself should be deemed miraculous. The beginning of the universe therefore is the end of science and naturalism.

Seeing such overwhelming evidence, many scientists have begun to believe in God, but they resort to deism. Even if science is unwilling to go beyond the empirical universe and admit the existence of a transcendent God, it must ascribe all the attributes of God to the universe and nature itself: that it created itself or existed eternally; that power, order, and wisdom are immanent in nature; that the laws of physics which bring about order in the universe are both omnipresent and omnipotent; and that they are omniscient enough to be fine-tuned and bring us into existence. Ironically, it is the very view that pantheism holds.

There are two ways in which deism can transition to theism—the origin of life and our free will. The origin of prokaryotes and eukaryotes—the atoms with which all life on earth is made of—has clear evidence of intelligent causation. These are William Paley's newest watches whose complexity implies a Watchmaker. The universe may be fine-tuned for sustaining life but it may not be enough to create life in the first place. An example might help: the functioning of an automobile engine can be reduced to physics and chemistry while its assembly cannot. Ditto in the case of life. We now know that life is not just physics and chemistry but also an information processing system. And all information systems are top-down design and not bottom-up.

Our free will is another miracle that we experience in our daily life. This makes our scientific enquiry "objective" and at the same time makes us morally responsible individuals. No physical system that is "nothing but" physics and chemistry can ever have free will. The present state of any physical system is the result of its previous state and the future is determined by its present. Yet we exercise free will every day of our lives and we have no clue how that can happen. If we leave aside the experimental difficulties in verifying whether we have free will or not, we must remember that scientific materialism cannot admit free will even in principle. And if they insist that we cannot have free will, then this debate is futile. They are shooting themselves in the foot by denying it. There cannot be any meaningful dialogue in the absence of free will. Unfortunately, even deism and pantheism cannot accommodate free will, which makes theism the most rationally consistent worldview of all.

Theism therefore is clearly a scientific and rational deduction. The greatest misunderstanding of this generation is that science validates atheism while the evidence is pointing to exactly the opposite direction. Atheism is simply not a viable option in context of the first cause. Denying God is denying the first cause which in turn is denying the scientific method of causality itself. Faith now seems redundant for this generation when we can rationally deduce the existence of God. Past generations who did not have the advancement of science may have needed faith to believe in God, but the current generation has no excuse because it has plenty of evidence pointing to a Creator who is powerful and intelligent. In the past, they needed miracles to be convinced, but for the present generation His ordinary works are more than sufficient. Whether one likes it or not, we are a product of an entity that miraculously created itself or had existed eternally.

Of all the three worldviews—theism, atheism, and agnosticism—it should be very clear to us that atheism and agnosticism are not even valid options. Denying the existence of our Creator is denying existence itself. Atheism is therefore the most unscientific and irrational position of all. And among all the three worldviews of belief—theism, deism, and pantheism—theism is clearly the most rationally consistent worldview of all. The only debate can now be on the nature of our Creator and not His existence.

Even if the atheists are not convinced with the solid evidence presented above, what does it take to rationalize their worldview? Plenty, as we shall see. The crucial point to note here is that we can believe in the existence of something with limited knowledge but cannot disbelieve while having half knowledge. Here is why: suppose we receive a radio signal which is transmitting the Newtonian equations, we can immediately conclude that Extra-Terrestrial Intelligence (ETI) exists without having to search further. For such believers in ETI the quest ends because they have limited but confirmed knowledge of their existence. They can now begin to speculate and debate on the nature of those aliens and cease from doubting their existence. Theism therefore is clearly justifiable in context of creation and fine-tuning of the universe.

But an atheist can never justify his unbelief until he has analyzed all the radio signals in the cosmos and found no intelligent signal among them. And for him to do that in space and time, analyzing signals from the past, present, and future, he would need to be omnipresent, omniscient, and omnipotent. We know that these are the very characters we attribute to God. In other words, it takes a God to say that there is no God. Humanity will do well by steering away from such hubris.

Many atheists boast that science is enough. Enough for what? Science is merely discovering how the universe works and not inventing it. Science is a puerile commentary of nature. Who or what invented the universe is the crucial question that every atheist has to answer and science with its causal methodology can never bail them out here. It is turtles all the way down for them.

Applied science takes the content of the universe—matter and the laws of physics that govern it—for granted. But atheism cannot afford to do that. Atheism has to begin with absolutely nothing and explain how everything came about. *Ex nihilio nihil fit!* (Out of nothing comes nothing.)

And if science takes its axioms and postulates for granted, then what is so great about its explanations? Give a toddler a bunch of Lego blocks with predefined rules of attaching them together and enough space and time in her crèche, she will more or less figure out all the permutations and combinations that exist.

We should remember that science itself is a product of two miracles. The miracle of universal order found in nature and the miracle of a free consciousness mind—the very tool used to explore that order in nature. Without the universal order that is found in nature, scientists would have been jobless cobblers. And without free will this debate is pointless.

Science may claim to be objective in its analysis but it is subjective with respect to its practitioners and their sensors. It is also subjective to the processing powers of its practitioners. Humans have a few sensors—eyes for sight, ears for sound, nose for smell, and skin for sensation. We can happily correlate information about these sensors until kingdom come, but that would in no way mean that is all there is in the universe. There can be no objective truths in science, only those which are subjective to its practitioners and the sensors that they possess, and science can never know what it does not know.

Consider the parable of the digicam—two digital cameras with light sensors can debate about the nature of reality, but are strictly limited to speak, theorize, and debate about light waves only. Now suppose a new digital camera is developed which has sensors to detect the dimension of time and sound—a video camera. The other two might scorn the new kid on the block and think it is deluded to hear sounds and perceive the extra dimension of time. They may even smartly shift the onus on the video camera to prove that something called "sound" exists. But unfortunately, the video camera may not have a processor which is smart enough to prove to others through a debate. It merely has a device that detects sound and a part of the processor is used to process and report that sound. In the end, the video camera will become more popular because of these new features and flourish while the other two will end up in the scrap heap.

Put spiritual experience in place of sound and you will know what we mean. Atheism is not only unscientific but is also against the very spirit of scientific inquiry. It is hypocritical of the atheists to be sceptical of one spiritual dimension (for which there is empirical evidence in the form of Near-Death Experiences recorded in the medical sciences throughout the world) while happily assuming seven more dimensions to justify string theory and its infinite landscape (for which there is not an iota of evidence.) All of these extra-dimensions to cover up the most embarrassing situation that prevails in the physics department— their inability to unify quantum physics with general relativity.

In the Christian worldview, God is a Spirit (John 4:24.) Science currently has no way of detecting conscious entities, how then does it plan to detect God? Neither can science figure out the contents of a conscious mind. It cannot even predict the trajectory of a fly, forget about comprehending the mind of God. The only way we can know what is in the mind of a conscious entity is by revelation. No one can know, even if they poke electrodes into my skull, if I would prefer strawberry over vanilla unless I choose to reveal it to them. Ditto for God. We can never know the contents of His mind unless He chooses to reveal it to us. And since God is not a "thing" but a person, it is His prerogative to reveal Himself to whomsoever He chooses—His saints and prophets. We ignore them at our peril.

One might be uncomfortable in believing divine revelation, but science is as much a divine revelation as religion. Unless the phenomenon reveals itself to us, we would have no clue about its existence. Dark matter and energy are grim reminders of this. Viewed this way, there is no difference between science and religion. Both are revelations. One is a revelation about nature and the other about the mind of God.

Every religion is characterized not only by a belief in God but also by its moral code. Jews have their Torah, the Buddhists have their Dhammapada, and the Christians have the Gospels. But where do atheists get their moral code from? If we delve a little deeper and search for the basis of their morality, it will become abundantly clear that this emperor has no clothes.

Anthony Grayling, the British philosopher, claims that there are no a-theists just as there are no a-stamp collectors (those who do not collect stamps as a hobby) and they will have nothing to say about God and religion until they have sufficient evidence to convince them. If we go by this logic, then they are a-moral as well, because there cannot be any moral code of conduct attached to a-stamp collectors.

It is a mistake to assume like many do, that atheism is equal to secular humanism. It is not. There is no connecting dot between them. Their worldview is devoid of any moral imperatives and will inevitably end up in nihilism or cynicism. Reason why some could even turn out to be Maoists or Communists. What about pyromaniacs claiming their right to gene expression? Who is to stop them and on what basis?

We can clearly see danger for humanity in an atheistic world which is morally ambiguous. Perhaps an example will help. Suppose there is a demented zoologist, let's call him HH Dawkins Dennett who is so enamoured by nature that he decides to eliminate humans, who he considers as pests that have drastically reduced the bio-diversity of the planet. He decides to target Asia, since that is where the maximum "pests" are located. We want to know which atheist or humanist in the West will step in to confront and stop him? And on what grounds? The atheistic worldview simply has nothing within its framework to stop this mad zoologist.

We have ample historical evidence that this has already happened in the past. Mao Zedong, one of the greatest mass-murderers in the history of mankind, thought such massacres will do well for China by reducing their population. His apathy clearly stems from his ignorance of the gospels.

Everybody talks about the twin towers these days but they seem to have conveniently forgotten the twin cities of Hiroshima and Nagasaki. And how a bunch of directionless scientists were drinking and dancing on the success of their new invention—the atom bomb—even as people were dying in those cities. They also conveniently forget how the twin super-powers—USA and former USSR—which were empowered by spineless scientists, have brought humanity to the brink of extinction because of the ideological differences they had during the cold war. Those who talk about the local chemist or pharmacist saving lives seem to have forgotten the chemists of Nazi Germany who committed the deadliest genocide in the history of mankind.

The real danger to humanity then is not religion, but science without a moral compass. Many think science has made religion redundant. We have just seen in the last century what will ensue if that happens. The two world wars had nothing to do with religion, yet caused immense suffering to mankind and large-scale destruction of Europe. All that mayhem was caused by the advance weaponry which scientists had developed without any moral scruples. This should teach us that we ignore religion at our peril.

If we define religion not only as a belief in God, but also one which has a code of conduct then we see no reason for religion to be redundant. Any society where it is taboo to point out its moral deficiencies is heading for dystopia. Religion has always been the conscience keeper of societies and nations. The churches in the west are empty not because they are lacking something, but because it demands a change in lifestyle. Unfortunately, that is exactly what is difficult for the present generation that has been brought up worshiping the Statue of Liberty as their mother goddess. Reason why we see moral degradation in schools and universities, in politics, and in the general society. We must remember that freedom comes with a responsibility.

In history, there is plenty of evidence on the positive role played by religion. Humanity has to thank religion for civilizing it. Ara Norenzayan notes that without religion, humanity would still be in stone ages (New Scientist: "God Issue: Religion is the key to civilization," dated March 2012.) Thankfully many atheists agree that Christianity has done immense good for humanity. But it is baffling to see Richard Dawkins deny that. Instead, he thinks it is culture that we have to thank. Does this bloke have any idea how local cultures pose the main obstacle for a universal ethical system? Has he even considered how inhumane certain cultures in the world are? According to the cultures of Africa and Papua New Guinea, there was nothing wrong with cannibalism. In India, it was considered virtuous for a widowed woman to join the funeral pyre of her husband and be burned alive. We can give countless such examples of dangerous practices throughout the world and all these cultural practices were blithely going on until the Christian missionaries arrived in those countries. Even the savage pre-Christian cultures of Europe like the Vikings and Visigoths were great impediments for the spread of Christianity. After Christianity established itself in Europe, local cultures and superstitions continued to corrupt the Church and made it depart from the essential teachings of Christ many times. Clear example of how local cultures make ethical systems parochial, subjective, and downright dangerous. It took a religion like Christianity to bring about a universal ethical system and unite mankind across races, cultures, and nations.

Which God? This question is often asked by every atheist as if it is some kind of ultimate gotcha, not realizing that atheism is infinitely more ambiguous than religion. We have already shown that humanism has nothing to do with atheism. Atheists could be cynics, nihilists, communists, or Maoists. Some are moral relativists while others are moral realists. Some believe in free will while the majority of them deny it. Some think science can determine human values while others deny it can do so.

There is ambiguity even in science. Sometimes there are multiple and contradictory theories that contend to explain a given phenomenon. As an example, there have been more theories and worldviews than the hair on my head which attempt to explain the "hard problem" of consciousness. Does that mean consciousness does not exist? That is being totally absurd. Or take the example of quantum physics, there are many who stand by the Copenhagen interpretation while others by the Austin interpretation. Some believe that reality does not exist at the subatomic level until it is measured, while others believe there are infinite parallel universes. Add to this confusion is another interpretation of John Wheeler—that of a participatory universe.

The great chain of delusion should be obvious to everyone by now: The neurologists think the biologists have it figured out, while the biologists think the chemists have it figured out, and the chemists think the physicists have it figured out, little realizing that the physicists have abandoned camp in the last century itself. In such a situation, science cannot even claim to know what the fundamental nature of reality is. There are multiple interpretations but no consensus even among the physicists. Which reality is science talking about then? In the same way, it is a *non sequitur* to claim that the true nature of God cannot be known just because there have been multiple attempts by humans to understand the mind of God. Just as in science, this is a failure of our intellect and not the phenomenon itself.

Science is also a work in progress that is trying to understand the ultimate nature of reality. We have shown earlier that although science may not vary in geography, it has varied tremendously in time. From claiming that earth, water, air, and fire are the basic elements to the standard model of atomic physics that is currently accepted today—it has been a long journey for science. And the standard model of atomic physics is certainly not a complete and perfect revelation of reality because there are many things that it has yet to answer. In the same way, no religion may have a fully accurate representation of God, but at least one will be a good working model. We should treat religions in the same way that we treat scientific and rational frameworks. In the end, any theory which is closest to truth should be accepted. In the same way, we believe only one religion to be closest to truth—Christianity.

When comparing religions, we could go on arguing until the cows come home because every religion has its proud moments and its embarrassing moments. Some believers set a good example and some don't. Every religion has its extremist elements too. It is very important therefore that we distinguish between what is done in the name of their religion and what is done according to their religion. This is very crucial when we do a comparative analysis of religions. Many embarrassing things have been done in the name of religion by the Klu Klux Klan, but a casual glance at the Gospels will show that it has been done in direct contradiction to the religion they profess. Instead of cherry-picking or quote mining the good or the bad parts, we should empirically look at what kind of societies that any given religion has nurtured in the long term.

Christ brilliantly gave another measure of verifying a true prophet. "Wherefore by their fruits ye shall know them." (Matthew 7:20.) We can clearly see what kind of fruits various religions of the world are bearing today. No one in their right mind would ever want to settle down in the Middle East which is ruled by Islamic orthodoxy. The same can be said of the Hindu caste divisions in rural India. And there is no counting as to how many in atheistic China desperately want to get out of their country. A clear indication that their religions (or lack of it) are untenable in the long run and the fruits they have borne are often very sad and unfortunate for those societies. Only Christianity has stood the test of time and has within it the doctrines of freedom, liberty, justice, and forbearance that mankind is searching for.

The church may have gone astray in the past but one cannot blame Christianity for everything that Christians do, especially if it is against the very code of conduct that they profess. And the reformation can only come from within and not outside of Christianity in the same way that any amendment needs to be consistent with the constitution of a country. Atheists have no business to point out to those lapses because they have no framework of their own. The atheists are the gun-toting outlaws here, who are harassing the law-abiding citizens.

It is true that the Church has violated the fundamental precepts of Christianity and has gone astray many a time, but these are mistakes that we should learn from. Any criticism of Christianity therefore should call for reformation and not elimination because the former is constructive while the latter is destructive. The clergy might have failed us, but Jesus Christ—the author and finisher of our faith—will never fail us. To give up religion just because a few clergymen have failed is like giving up on the constitution and deciding to be outlaws just because of a few corrupt officials. Nothing can be more counterproductive. Instead, we need to reinforce our commitment to Christianity and pray for the clergy and encourage them in their difficult ministry. The clergy may not be infallible, but they are least likely to be wrong in the same way a doctor, an engineer, or a lawyer are least likely to be wrong in their respective fields.

Of course, there are problematic passages in the Bible, we are not denying that, but there are problematic equations in science too. Why pick one and let the other go scot free? If it is "God of the gaps" then in it is also "atheism of the gaps."

Since the atheists have no ethical framework, all their "why" questions tend to be whimsical. We confess that we have no pretensions of knowing all the answers to their questions, but we know out of experience that no answer we give will ever satisfy these eternal pessimists because of their bias. At the same time, we also believe that no answer can ever nullify the other powerful evidence of God that we already have in context of the creation of our cosmos and life.

The "why" questions therefore are neither scientific nor rational questions. They cannot be scientific because the scientists themselves term such questions irrelevant. We must accept the phenomena as it is and not how we whimsically want it to be. In the same way, if they don't like the nature of God as revealed in the Bible, then that is still no reason to deny His existence.

They cannot be rational because one cannot answer questions of a given rational framework in an entirely different one. For example, one cannot ask Christianity to rationalize the Epicurean concepts of well-being. In mathematics, no one applies the rules of set theory to do calculus.

One of their favourite "why" questions is the problem of suffering. With this, they subtly appeal to emotions rather than the intellect of the audience. They ask the audience how a good God could allow such pain and suffering that we see in the world. For us, this is a theological question that has been answered two millennia ago by the Apostles and the early church fathers who experienced more suffering and persecution than can be imagined in the present world. But if those theological answers do not satisfy the atheists, then they should not be asking such theological questions in the first place. On one hand, the atheists refuse to see any value in theology, yet hypocritically raise theological questions and assume it can never be answered.

If they are rejecting the existence of a "good" God then how do they know that He is not good in the first place? We have already pointed out that the only way of knowing a person's mind is via revelation. God of the Bible has revealed Himself to be a compassionate God in many passages of the Bible (Jeremiah 9:23-24) and also by laying down His very life for humanity, but the atheists seem to think they are some super psychologists who know God more than He knows Himself! The howl of the Rottweiler is a textbook example of this hubris (see *The God Delusion*, chapter two, first para.) Such strident conclusions of the atheists on the nature of God are absurd and unwarranted. Terry Eagleton reviewing *The God Delusion* had this to say: Imagine someone holding forth on biology whose only knowledge of the subject is the Book of British Birds, and you have a rough idea of what it feels like to read Richard Dawkins on theology.

A religion cannot profess to be propagating truth when its foundations are mythical, no matter how profound the philosophical insights are in its mythological books. If we remove all the religions that are founded on myths then only a few handful contenders of truth will be left. And among the historical ones, a strong case can be made for ethical monotheism.

All the three Abrahamic religions are historical and ethical monotheistic. Ironically, Jesus Christ is mentioned in scriptures of all the three of them. In the Old Testament, which the Jews follow, there are prophecies of a messiah who will come in the end times, which the Christians believe will be Jesus in His second coming (in fact, the messianic Jews already believe in Jesus.) And in the Quran, Jesus is already venerated as a prophet who will return. If there is a single person who has the potential to unite all the three Abrahamic faiths then it is none other than Jesus Christ himself.

Fifty-three people mentioned in the Old Testament have extra-Biblical evidence that they have existed. Fourteen of these include kings of Israel and Judah who are mentioned in the two books of Kings. New evidence is emerging on complexes built by David in Khirbet Qeiyafa and defensive walls built by Solomon in Jerusalem. Even the pools of Siloam (where Jesus healed the blind man) and Bethesda have been unearthed in Jerusalem.

Coming to the evidence from the time of Jesus, twenty-three people (mainly political figures) mentioned in the New Testament including Pontius Pilate and Caiaphas the High Priest (both of whom were involved in crucifying Jesus) have extra-Biblical evidence that they have existed. There is also strong circumstantial evidence that we have discovered the House of Peter in Capernaum (that was later converted into a place of worship) and the childhood home of Jesus in Nazareth (or what the earliest Christians believed it to be when they built a Byzantine church on it.)

No other ancient religion has such archaeological evidence to support its authenticity. Since they cannot ignore such important archaeological evidence, atheists now change their strategy and claim that the Bible is historical fiction. They admit that the people and places mentioned in the Bible are true, but demand evidence of the narrative itself. This reeks of double standards in context of abiogenesis and a universe which is supposed to have popped out of absolutely nothing. We are not sure how much more evidence is needed to convince them. Do they expect us to go back in time and get a video recording of all the events recorded in the Bible? Jesus was right about not bothering to present any more evidence to such eternal pessimists, "…neither will they be persuaded, though one rose from the dead." (Luke 16:31.)

Dan Barker literally fulfils the prophecy of Jesus by saying that even if it were proven that Jesus rose from the dead, it would still not mean that He is the Son of God. Well, in that case even the fossils don't prove evolution. They are just bones of dead animals. Such extreme scepticism of the atheists can even relapse into solipsism—how do we know that we are not just a brain in a vat? We cannot even begin to do our science with confidence under such circumstances.

Recorded history of the Gospels has much more probability of being true than speculations of pre-history like abiogenesis. We still have no clue how life itself arose. We have no clue if natural selection is enough to account for the major transitions of life and all its complexity. The origin of species is trivial compared to the problem of the origin of phyla seen during the Cambrian explosion. Yet the atheists have blind faith that all of the above do not need intelligent causation. How do they know that?

The atheists are not only bad in science and rationality but also in interpreting history. In his book *The New Atheist Denial of History*, Borden W. Painter clearly shows how the atheists have distorted history. He points out the lack of historical credibility in their claims when compared to the conventional criteria used by mainstream historians.

There is plenty of convergent evidence in the gospels that Christ claimed to be divine. Most atheists think we should not trust the gospels because they were written by believers decades later. But that is putting the cart before the horse. How did they come to be believers in the first place? Even before the gospels were written, Christianity spread like wild fire in the Mediterranean region. On the flip side, if we apply the same logic to the books on evolution, we should be dumping all of those in the dustbin too, since they are all written by believers in evolution millions of years after the events are supposed to have taken place.

The best source of evidence are eyewitnesses. Even judges and historians always rely on eyewitnesses. The authors of the synoptic gospels had gathered data from such eyewitnesses (I Corinthians 15:6.) There may be minor differences in chronology and circumstances within the synoptic gospels but none of them affect the central doctrines of Christianity and what Jesus said about Himself. We must remember that these gospels were written in separate places by different people and yet there is remarkable agreement between them. This itself should attest to the reliability of the information found in the gospels.

Even scepticism needs to be rationalized. If there was only one eyewitness who was drunk, then we have reasons to be sceptical. But if there were multiple sober witnesses then we have no rational reason to doubt. And if the witness himself was a sceptic like Saint Paul then there is absolutely no reason to doubt. The problem with most of the sceptics is when the gospels agree verbatim, they assume it was copied from another common source even while having no evidence to present for such an assumption. Why not interpret the similarity by assuming multiple sources that witnessed an authentic common event?

We should also remember that the early Christians were anything but blind believers, although there were disagreements between them on which books were authentic, yet all of them ratified the gospels we currently find in the New Testament. While the synoptic gospels give facts and figures, the Gospel of Saint John gives the most accurate theological interpretation of what happened in history. We have reasons to believe that the source of information for this gospel was the youngest disciple of Jesus (and the last to die) who had enough time to reflect and interpret what Jesus said and did.

Historians generally agree that the baptism of Jesus, the appointing of the disciples, His criticism of Levitical priesthood, and His subsequent crucifixion by the Romans have indeed taken place in history. They have increasing difficulty in separating the ministry of Jesus with the miracles He performed, which shows that miracles were integral to His ministry. To this general consensus, we would like to add the resurrection. We know from historical records that the early Christians were expecting Jesus to return any moment during their lives to the extent that they sold everything they had and donated it to the Church and lived as a community. If Jesus was dead and his bones were still around, who were they expecting to return? If Saul wanted to bust Christianity, he just needed to show them the tomb of Jesus with His bones in it. Instead, we have the testimony regarding the resurrection from Christianity's enemy number one. What more evidence can we ask for than the testimony of one who was against Christianity itself?

The Holy Bible is not a book of physics, chemistry, or biology. I am not sure how the atheists miss that. Instead, it is looking at history and civics from a theological perspective. As a broad historical summary, the Bible is spot on in revealing what science currently knows. Set in its time, the creation narrative was light years ahead of others including the Greeks. We now know that the universe had a definitive beginning and is not eternal as Aristotle envisaged, that the diversity of life was created in different stages, and that man—who was made out of the elements of the earth—was the last to come. Homo became Sapiens (wise) on the day he understood that his Creator must necessarily exist and began to call upon His name (Gen 4:26.) Unfortunately, many these days are becoming atavistic and are randomly mutating back to Homo Stupidus!

Anyone out there still arguing whether it took six days or billions of years for the creation of this universe and life are outdated in their physics by a century, or do not seem to have a full understanding of the theory of relativity. We now know that it is pointless to talk about absolute time. According to the theory of relativity, space and time are intertwined. We cannot separate one from the other and according to the Bible, a great gulf separates humanity from God (Luke 16:26) who is the first cause and the source of all creation.

We will now examine what the atheists have said during the debate and expose their scientific and rational pretentions.

The prayer on Higgs boson is a caricature that only the facile atheists can come up with. Scientists had reasonable faith that Higgs Boson exists, exactly why they sunk billions of dollars into it. It took decades for them to build the LHC and detect the Higgs boson. Ditto for God. It takes a lifetime to prepare ourselves to meet our God. Like the atheist, we don't lazily sit on the veranda and issue a habeas corpus for God to appear and give evidence.

According to the Christian worldview, God is not a thing but a person. It is His prerogative to reveal Himself to whomsoever He wills—His saints and prophets—we ignore them at our peril.

We sincerely hope that the atheists are not thrusting electrodes into the heads of their spouses to seek evidence of their love. This is no way to develop a relationship. Ditto with God. If we have to develop a relationship with Him then we need to have faith and trust on Him. While it takes observation and experiments to build gadgets and cars, it takes faith and trust to build meaningful relationships between people and nations.

Talking about free will, Barker himself admits that they there is no consensus among the atheists on this. This should actually be a no-brainer for them specially when one of their prophets calls us lumbering robots. The atheists simply cannot afford free will in a materialistic bottom-up view of the universe. In such a worldview what objective science can you expect? What universal truths can we expect from a calculator built to crunch numbers? None whatsoever. If atheism is right then atheism is wrong.

As mentioned earlier, the problem of evil and suffering is a flawed argument because nobody rejects the noun because they don't like the adjectives. Even if our answers to this problem does not satisfy the atheists, we are open to debate on the true nature of God, but they should first admit that there is no debate about His existence because the first cause is a scientific and rational deduction beyond debate.

It is also wrong to assume that this life is meant to be a pleasure trip. It is not. It is rather a dispensation of grace given for repentance. In the Christian worldview, the suffering in this world and the dismal state of nature is exactly what one would expect when the creation has departed from the presence of God. We are a brilliant creation that have fallen from grace. The desire of atheists to have all pleasure and no pain is totally irrelevant to the existence of God. In this context, we see no difference between a Islamic jihadi and the atheist. The former is accepting God for the pleasure of meeting seventy-two virgins in the afterlife and the latter is denying the existence of God because he is denied that pleasure in this life itself.

Michael Shermer takes us through various social, evolutionary, and psychological factors that have led us to believe in God. If the rustle in the grass led me to believe in God then why don't the apes have a God? They too face the same challenges. If religion is a social construct then maybe atheism is a western construct of a secular society. If I believe because I have a God "gene" then maybe they disbelieve because they lack one. If I believe because of a chemical in my brain called "theistocin," then maybe they have a deficiency of the same, or an excess of a chemical called "atheistoxin." How come they believe they are some superior beings who have gone over and above their physics and chemistry? And that too in direct contradiction to their worldview that we are nothing but chemical scum? We will have nothing to do with such elitist flapdoodle. Any materialistic explanation that applies to theism will apply to atheism as well.

Shermer asks how likely is it for Christianity to be right among many other religions found in the world. Well, using the same logic how likely is atheism true compared to the believers who believe in a Creator God? They are a pathetic minority. And if the majority are more likely to be true then the Abrahamic religions which constitute a great majority must be true.

When pointing to the fact that all early pioneers of science were committed Christians, Michael Shermer shrugs it off saying that they were people of their times. If we use the same logic, then maybe the atheists are the people of their times too—born in a godless secular society.

Dominus Illuminatio Mea, says the motto of this esteemed institution. It translates to "The Lord is my Light." Let it continue to be so. As of today, as you vote "with your legs," all of you are free to go through either the "Nay" or the "Aye" door but as far as I am concerned: I protest. I will instead choose the fire exit because I do not believe that truth can be decided by a Gallup poll. And depending on the result, I will either continue to hold this institution in high esteem, or lose all respect for it and call it a den of fools. Just as it has been said in Romans 1:22 "...professing to be wise, they have become fools..."

FREQUENTLY ASKED STUPID QUESTIONS

In this section, we answer a few Frequently Asked stupid Questions which every atheist repeats like a parrot.

Question: Who created God?

Great question, but I think that this question is irrelevant to the point of discussion. If I were an alien who stumbled upon the Curiosity rover on Mars, then I would conclude that it was created by some clever and wise entity for a purpose, even if I had no clue about earthlings, or may never know how the earthlings came to be in the first place. For us, the complexity of a living cell is a clear indication of intelligent causation.

We should instead rephrase the question: Who created us? Definitely not ourselves. We all know that science gives facile answers by pointing to the immediate preceding causes. But the causal chain is as strong as its weakest link and we will eventually trace it to the first cause. The first cause therefore is the root cause of my existence.

Science currently tells us that it takes tremendous "power" in the form of energy, "order" in the form of the laws of physics, and "wisdom" to fine-tune those laws of physics to create a universe that can go on to create us. And this power, order, and wisdom either came through the first cause (Big Bang) or existed forever as an eternal source. Whatever science chooses to label the first cause or the eternal source of all creation, we revere that entity as our Creator God.

This conclusion is inevitable. Faith is no longer needed when we can deduce a clear rational proof of God who created us. Either God created Himself and then created us or He exists eternally. How He could do that is a profound mystery which we have no pretensions of knowing.

It is the atheist who is irrational to believe that the universe came out of absolutely nothing. This claim can neither be scientific nor rational and borders on the nonsensical. Even if scientists don't want to extrapolate anything beyond what we see, feel, or touch, they will have to end up as pantheists. They could not have existed without matter and the laws that govern them. Scientists have inadvertently become the high priests of natural theology.

It is logically impossible to be atheistic in a causal world, once we know that we did not create ourselves. The first cause or the eternal source is a brute fact that science cannot ignore. They have to take at least one principle for granted, and for us that is "In the beginning was the Word..." (John 1:1.)

Every human endeavor of comprehension takes for granted certain unprovable or irreducible axioms and postulates. Mathematics has its own set of axioms and postulates. Science takes for granted matter and the laws that govern it as its axioms and postulates without explaining how they came about in the first place. Why then should the atheists object if theists take God as their axiom and postulate? Even if we are unable to explain how He came to be in the first place.

We must remember that "Does God exist?" and "Who created God?" are two mutually exclusive questions. Just because we cannot answer the second question does not mean that God does not exist. A cartoon animation character can rationally credit its creator for animating it, even while having no clue how the Creator himself came into being.

<u>Question: Which God?</u>

It is a *non sequitur* to say God does not exist just because there are so many religions in the world. In science, no one discounts a phenomenon just because there are multiple theories attempting to explain it. For example, there are as many theories as the hair on my head which are attempting to explain the "hard problem" of consciousness. But does that mean consciousness does not exist? Not at all.

Christianity has used the same method of truth and logic to convert Europe from its myth based paganism that men of science use to prove their theories today. Early Christianity had many apologists who wrote volumes to convince and convert those who were believing in myths. Not sure why the atheist are trying to reinvent the wheel here. Just as in science, where any one among many theories qualifies in the end, we believe that any one religion will be closest to truth even if it may not have a full and perfect revelation—for us that is Christianity.

Why Christianity alone? We have many reasons to believe in it. Any religion that is propagating truth cannot have myths as its foundation. By this Occam's razor, we eliminate all the false ones and just a few remain. Among the remaining, the ethical monotheistic ones stand distinctly apart as being the most coherent. Abrahamic religions are both historical and ethically monotheistic. And Christ is the only one who claimed divinity among all the three Abrahamic religions.

The irony is that Christ figures in all the three Abrahamic religions—as a future prophet of the Jews, as a Son of God for the Christians, and as a venerated prophet in Islam. If there is anyone who can unite the world then Jesus Christ alone can and will.

Of course, there may be many unanswered questions and contradictions in Christianity. But that is also the case in science and philosophy. Why single out Christianity then? If it is "God of the gaps" then it is also "atheism of the gaps."

On the flip side, we could ask the same question to the atheists. Which atheism are they talking about? Epicurean? Cynical? Nihilistic? Communist? Maoist? One which does not believe in free will? Or one which says science has nothing to do with ethics? Or the one which says it can? One which believes that we are nothing but chemical scum or lumbering robots? Or the one that thinks that they are demigods with free will who can transcend their own brains to rationalize and do objective science?

Atheistic Statement: "God did it" explains nothing.

This is an absurd statement usually made by atheists like Lawrence Krauss. But of all people, he should know better that God explains infinitely more than "nothing," the supposed "thing" that everything is presumed to have come from. God explains where the power, order, and wisdom needed to create this universe came from.

Ironically, it is exactly what we think about the theory of evolution—that it explains absolutely nothing. It begins with the worst premise in the history of science: Given time and chance, anything can happen. It assumes the very thing that it is supposed to explain, a complex self-replicating living organism. No one has any clue how life began while the evolutionists blithely take it for granted as the starting point of their theory. They still have no clue how all the major transitions of life came about. The transition of unicellular organisms to multicellular ones, asexual to sexual reproduction, and the complex brain are all explained away as "miracles of evolution" (the second greatest oxymoron mankind has ever known.) Our consciousness too is attributed to evolution even while they are struggling to comprehend it. And by evolution what they really mean is "natural selection of innovations that arose by sheer dumb luck!"

It is unscientific and irrational to believe that evolution is enough to explain all complexity, even when we have no clue what is needed for something like life or consciousness to arise. Instead, these atheistic assertions are based on blind faith which we reject with a firm conviction.

Even if God had created the universe, Michael Shermer asks us why we would not want to know how God did it, for the sake of science. If God did it, then I would not waste time in finding out how He did it, but would like to know from Him why He did it. I would like to know His eternal purpose for me. The "how" question then becomes secondary.

Atheistic statement: We neither believe in God nor in Zeus, Thor, flying spaghetti monster, leprechauns, or tooth fairies.

Trivialize and dismiss is the modus operandi of the militant atheists. No one in their right mind believes in tooth fairies in this day and age—or for that matter even three millennia back. The Abrahamic religion which is the foundation of Christianity had rejected all such primitive conceptions of God long ago. Christians were even called atheists by Romans exactly because they did not believe in such ridiculous conceptions of God like Zeus, Thor, or Venus. It is disingenuous of the atheists to rake up such primitive concepts of God to dismiss the Abrahamic religions. It is like ridiculing modern-day science by looking at the history of science when they believed that the earth was the center of the universe and that everything is made of four elements (earth, fire, water, and air.)

Ironically, they are the ones who believe in flying spaghetti monsters, but call them with slightly different names: Derkolo, Ewok, Chewbacca, Spock, and little green men. Search for Extra-Terrestrial Intelligence is based on the blind faith that there must be aliens out there, even when they don't have a shred of empirical evidence to prove that. Few even believe in celestial teapots, but call them flying saucers. NASA has even spent billions in sending probes and rovers to Mars with exactly this wild speculation based on blind faith.

Question: Does not bad design found in nature prove that God did not create them?

There are four reasons why a few bad designs found in nature do not negate the existence of intelligent causation. Firstly, it is a statistical no-brainer. For every supposed bad design they point to, we can show a hundred brilliant designs. Good design wins hands down on a statistical table. Secondly, it is more rational to believe that the less optimized designs are the result of low priority than to believe the highly optimized ones came about by blind chance.

Thirdly, if I were an engineer who made a robot with such great intelligence that it can optimize and improve its own functionality, then I would be considered an extraordinary genius. Ditto for human design by God. By pointing to deficient design, they have just increased my respect for the design of my brain which spotted that in the first place. And this is inversely proportional, the more I see scope for improvement, the more it reinforces my respect for the good design of my brain.

Lastly, it is a self-defeating argument. If bad design is evidence that God does not exist, then our brain must also have been formed by some unguided random processes and therefore all its conclusions need to be thrown out of the window—including that of bad design. They should discard their other conclusions also, including atheism.

Richard Dawkins mocks and ridicules God by pointing to the extra length of laryngeal nerve of a giraffe. For us, it is like a person going into a complex data centre (the brain) and after checking out all the complicated networks, switches, routers, and firewalls, decides that it could not have been designed because he saw some extra cable somewhere. This is being petty to the power of infinity!

Question : *What about slavery?*

The Old Testament clearly instructs the Children of Israel to free the slaves on the seventh year. Many atheists seem to be completely misguided in thinking that Christianity is silent about slavery. In this, they are no better than the early Americans of the south. Jesus Christ himself speaks about another kind of slavery—a spiritual one—which is more important than the literal one. Man is born free, but everywhere he is in bondage of sin.

Michael Shermer and the other atheists give endless homilies on slavery without even getting the basics right. How do the atheists know that slavery is wrong? What is the basis of their judgement? As we have shown earlier in the book that atheism is also amoral since it has no constitution to base its judgement on. Not that I am claiming that slavery is right, but I am curious to know how they have come to judge the right from the wrong without an ethical framework of their own.

If the claims of a strong Artificial Intelligence are right (that machines will one day become conscious) then even my car could become conscious one day. Will they begin to penalize me for using it as a slave to get me around? We should be giving up all such devices in that case. Richard Dawkins claims that humans are "nothing but" lumbering robots programmed by their genes to survive ruthlessly. If so, then we are enslaved by our own genes. If the reductionists are right then consciousness is an irrelevant sensation of the brain which in turn is nothing but molecules in motion. Pray what freedom, liberty, and justice can they proclaim in such a worldview?

Daniel Dennett and Michael Shermer speculate several theories on how free will can be achieved. Their speculations are just creative imaginations of those who have still no clue about what consciousness is. Such sophistry will not do. Their books are popular best sellers and not peer-reviewed scientific papers. It is impossible for free will to arise in their reductionist worldview, even in principle.

Besides all this, why do atheists now want the Church to interfere with governance? It was a common Roman practice to own slaves. Did they want the Christian churches to take charge of the Roman governance? If yes, then why not now? Especially when it is greatly needed in the scientific community, who have ravaged the planet and are driving humanity to the brink of extinction.

On the flip side, if the secularists don't want the church to interfere with the state then the state should not interfere with religious injunctions as well. The state has no right to force churches to solemnize gay marriages.

Question : What about virgin birth and resurrection of Jesus Christ? And miracles in general?

The fundamental question about virgin birth and resurrection is about miracles. If a sufficiently advanced technology of man is indistinguishable from miracles then maybe miracles mentioned in the Bible are exactly that. If man, who is made in the image of God can do it with technology, then why not God? If man can manage to do cloning and revive patients on the threshold of death, then why not God? When intelligence is around, anything is possible and we have plenty of evidence of that intelligence in context of fine-tuning of the laws of physics.

If they think the virgin birth and resurrection are absurd claims then so are abiogenesis and the theory that universe popped out of absolutely nothing. How come they are willing to believe energy, matter, laws, and constants of nature can pop out of nothing? How come they believe that life can self-assemble from a broth of chemicals zapped with the magic wand of lightning? If resurrection seems absurd then the claim that machines will be resurrected with consciousness is equally absurd.

We have already shown in the chapter on naturalism that existence itself at the fundamental level is preternatural. It no longer makes any sense to differentiate the normal and the miraculous when nature itself is a miracle.

Question : What about hellfire?

Reminder: This is not a scientific question but a theological one. And the answer has already been given in the Holy Bible. God created hell for Satan and his angels, and not for mankind. "Then shall He say also unto them on the left hand, Depart from me, ye cursed, into everlasting fire, prepared for the devil and his angels:" (Matthew 25:41.) But if one out of his own free will wants to follow Satan into that place then that is his lookout. Don't tell us that we did not warn you.

If a loving mother tells her child not to play with fire, the atheists are more bothered about protocol than about the sad consequences of a child playing with fire. A typical case of shooting the messenger. God sent his only begotten son to rescue us from that fire. Ignore Him at your peril.

Science also tells us that we will be consumed along with our planet in a lake of fire when the sun expands rapidly after exhausting its fuel. Is anybody rejecting science because of this true revelation simply because it is uncomfortable? Why then should we reject the Bible for revealing uncomfortable truths about the future of all those who choose evil over good?

The atheists are in this matter worse that the Islamic jihadists. While the latter is causing temporary suffering on this earth for the pleasure of seventy-two virgins, the former are setting humanity up for eternal suffering because they are denied that pleasure in this life itself.

Question : Should we have faith?

The first sin of Adam and Eve was to distrust what God told them. Satan deceived mankind and brought about a deep mistrust between man and God. Adam had plenty of evidence of God but what he lacked was trust. Contrary to popular concept of faith, God gave plenty of empirical evidence to the Israelites and to the disciples of Jesus. We see that evidence in many places in the Bible. The Israelites were the original sceptics who always demanded signs and wonders. Jesus himself healed many sick and raised the dead but what Saint Thomas lacked was trust in the words of Jesus when He said He would rise from death on the third day. The rebuke that followed was therefore justified.

As pointed out earlier, we have to trust one another to have a meaningful relationship. I hope the atheists are not thrusting electrodes into the skulls of their spouses to verify their love or asking them to undergo lie detector tests every time they profess their love for them. This is no way to build a relationship. Ditto with God.

While science gathers knowledge, faith garners trust. What the current world needs is not knowledge or science but faith and trust between wife and husband, parents and children, families and the clergy, people and leaders, and between nations. Another reason why we need Christianity more than ever.

Question: What about natural disasters?

Reminder: This is not a scientific question but a theological one. According to Christian theology, natural disasters are of two types. One is divine retribution when mankind strays away from truth and the other is Satan's doing with evil intent and purpose. In the former, God sends His prophets to give sufficient warning and time to repent, failing which disaster strikes for the greater good of mankind. But the latter takes mankind by utter surprise.

Although God created this magnificent cosmos, He gave mankind the free will to choose between good and evil. Unfortunately, mankind voted God out of their lives and elected Satan to rule their lives. Christ Himself said that in John 18:36 "My kingdom is not of this world." And in John 14:30 "For the *prince of this world* cometh, and he hath nothing in me." All sicknesses, suffering, and natural disasters come through Satan, reason why Jesus always rebuked sicknesses and natural disasters in Mark 4:39, "And he arose, and rebuked the wind, and said unto the sea, Peace, be still. And the wind ceased, and there was a great calm."

But why does God not judge and eliminate Satan to stop natural disasters? That is in His agenda—Revelation 20:10. But true to His nature, He will begin that judgement first from His own house and that would mean that He will have to judge humanity along with Satan. Instead, He sent His only begotten Son on a rescue mission to salvage humanity first and fulfil the eternal purpose that He had for them—to make them his own sons and daughters and co-heirs of His creation. Satan will be judged soon after that and thereby ending all suffering, sickness, and natural disasters. "Thy kingdom come. Thy will be done in earth, as it is in heaven." (Mathew 6:10.)

Question: *What about religious violence?*

The true enemy of humanity is man himself and his evil nature. And there is currently only one institution on the planet that recognizes this and is trying to reform him, that is religion. Christianity to be precise. Not all religions believe that we are evil and fallen by nature. While science is dangerously arming man with guns and grenades, in spite of knowing his evil nature.

True to his evil nature, man will inevitably resort to violence and justify it. And this justification could be religion, nationalism, ideology, or plain skin colour. The two world wars had nothing to do with religion, yet caused large-scale destruction and immense suffering to mankind. If that were not

213

enough, the ideological differences between capitalists and communists have brought humanity to the brink of extinction during the cold war.

But if violence has taken place in the name of Christianity, then it has happened in direct contradiction to what Christ preached. What matters is not whether violence was committed in the name of religion, but whether it was committed according to religion. Under no circumstances is violence allowed in Christianity—Christ Himself set a brilliant example for us. A Christian departs from his religion the instant he resorts to violence. In that brief moment, his evil nature takes over and he becomes an atheist who is not governed by any ethical framework or thinks he can hoodwink God and rationalize it. The Church has struggled in Europe to reform the likes of Vikings and Visigoths who were barbaric and ruthless to the core. It was quite a task to get them to accept the doctrine of forgiveness preached by Christ. Don't muzzle the ox while it is treading the corn. This continues to be a work in progress of the church.

Question: What about suffering in the world?

Once again, we have to remind the atheists that the problem of suffering is a theological question and not a scientific one. And the early church fathers had answered it two millennia ago. If the atheists are not convinced by those answers, then they should not be asking theological questions.

According to the Bible, suffering in the world is exactly what we should expect to see when it is devoid of God's presence. The fallen man is cast out from the presence of God and a great gulf (of space and time) separates them (Luke 16:26.) The earth is also cursed due to man's disobedience. And since man has voted to be ruled by God's adversary—Satan, he rules with disastrous consequences.

Funnily, the atheists seem to say that if God gives every human a grand mansion, a cute spouse, trouble-free children, and loads of cash in the bank then they will believe that he is a good God (Michael Shermer says he will believe Him if 10 million were credited into his account.) But this is patently absurd. The purpose of creation is not for humans to take a pleasure trip but something of higher value. According to the Bible, God wants to train us to be His children and inherit all that He has. Suffering has a definitive and important purpose because without it, we would not know how to empathise. How can a pastor pray for a child who has a toothache without experiencing it himself? How will one stop doing what pains others without undergoing that pain oneself? Christians the world over understand this fundamental truth, except of course those who live in Oxford. It's one reason why it is the Christians who are more proactive in alleviating suffering wherever they see it, instead of sulking like the athcists. Precisely why a Christian mother who lost all her three children in the tsunami that hit costal Tamil Nadu in India, adopted thirty more who had lost their parents, instead of whining like the atheists. Reason why Christian organizations are ready to alleviate suffering anywhere in the world. Reason why people prefer to be treated in Christian hospitals which are much more compassionate and humane than the commercial hospitals. Reason why countless clergy have given up all they have in order to serve God and humanity.

While Islam is sending suicide bombers to take the life of others, we are sending missionaries who lay down their life for others. When the Hindus and the Buddhists are blaming the karma of previous life for leprosy, Christian missionaries are washing, cleaning, and feeding lepers to alleviate their suffering. I wish Christopher Hitchens were still around. I would have personally knocked the living daylights out of him for maligning Mother Teresa of India.

It is time atheists stop lazing around in their ivory towers and come to see the ground reality in India where even the Muslims and the Hindus revere schools and hospitals run by Christian missionaries.

Atheistic statement: We have to keep God out of the school curriculum.

One of the most unfortunate decisions that the founders of the American nation have taken is to remove God from their political and education systems in the name of secularism. This was perhaps influenced by the violent history of Europe. But why should such aberrations influence the affairs of a state or get in the way of our quest for truth? What happens when science discovers unmistakable evidence of intelligent causation like the fine-tuning of the initial conditions? Would they not call for a press conference if they detected Extra-Terrestrial Intelligent signals? Why then have they not called for a press conference when the fine-tuning dawned on the physicists? If someone finds authentic archaeological evidence of the Ark of the Covenant, would they cease teaching about that in history classes just because colleges are supposed to be secular? If a university is to teach unbiased truth to the students then they cannot afford to keep God out of their curriculum. In such a scenario, to be "secular" is being against the quest for truth.

Because God is kept out of this quest, universities are becoming increasingly dogmatic about their materialistic position in spite of where the evidence is pointing to. Truth-seeking students are unfortunately stifled by such materialistic dogma in spite of overwhelming evidence of intelligent causation found in nature. By doing this, the universities have departed from a sincere quest for truth, and they cease to go boldly where the evidence leads them. I thank God that I don't have children. I would never have sent them to these western madrassas called universities which are churning out materialistic and atheistic fundamentalists.

On one hand, we are imparting deep knowledge of nature to our children in the universities and on the other not guiding them to use it with empathy for the benefit of mankind. Reason why they join the weapons industry without any moral scruples, or go after corporates for short-term gain without thinking twice. This is not a holistic education. It is time we change the constitution of America because science without a moral compass is a real and present danger for mankind.

The need of the hour for mankind is not scientific progress but a religious revival. Science may have given us earthly comforts (of course there is no such thing as a free lunch, such comforts are only for the rich who can afford it) but we should not allow the greed of nations and corporates to ransack the earth. While thanking science half-heartedly for giving us those comforts, we dismiss it. Can the scientists step aside and make room for the clergy please?

In history, religion has guided the original quest for truth. Ethics and morals are the sole provinces of religion. Why not teach different religious thoughts to our children in school and let them decide? Let the parents be ready to present rational reasons for their commitment to a certain religion and let the child decide when she grows up. Let there be open debates and conversions between religions and let us learn from history to keep violence out in our quest for truth and God. The majority religion of every country should allow open debates and discussion on different religions and allow one to freely convert. The greatness of any nation can be easily judged by how it treats the minorities.

Viewed from outer space, we can see no borders on our planet. All national borders are manmade, preventing them from being united across the globe as a single nation under our Creator. God is neither parochial, nor petty to be restricted to any single country. Our Creator is the creator of this entire universe. No state or national boundaries can withhold him. Nationalism therefore should cease to be a virtue—it is no longer cool to be parochial. Since truth cannot be plural, there is only one God and one religion and it is the duty of mankind to search for that one true religion and God and accept them without letting their national or ideological ego get in the way. Truth knows no boundaries and true religion spans across countries and continents: There is neither Jew nor Greek, there is neither bond nor free, there is neither male nor female: for ye are all one in Christ Jesus (Galatians 1:28.)

Unfortunately, many countries persecute the minority. Muslims want democracy and equal rights where they are a minority and want the Sharia implemented where they are a majority. Such double standards won't do. Rome has set a fine example by allowing a mosque to be built within its city limits. It is time for Saudi Arabia to reciprocate and open the gates of Mecca for Christian missionaries. There is no fear in truth but a lot of insecurity in falsity. Only cowards are afraid of conversion.

Question: Should religion concern itself with scientific theories?

Religion should not subscribe, profess, or promote any scientific theory because they are all ephemeral. We should learn from our past mistakes. Ptolemaism was cutting-edge science in the early Christian centuries and the church was so enamoured by it that it began to include it in its teachings. We all know the unfortunate results that followed.

Science continually upgrades to newer versions. At any given point of time, a science textbook will have quite a few outdated elements in it. For science, this is a never-ending story. Their reductionist worldview leads to a *reductio ad absurdum*: "Ever learning, and never able to come to the knowledge of the truth." (II Timothy 3:7.)

But science should unambiguously interpret evidence without their materialistic bias. If they have found evidence of God's existence then they should be courageous enough to state the truth, regardless of the consequences. If they do that, then it would be the scientists who would be leading the revival meetings as true witnesses of His incredible power and wisdom in the universe. Unfortunately, the academia is so hung up on materialism that they go to the extent of believing the ridiculous claim of Lawrence Krauss that the universe came out of absolutely nothing. Truth has flown away from the corridors of today's universities.

Question: What use is Theology?

Lawrence Krauss questions theology and wants to know what knowledge it has given us? This is a flawed question. Theology is not a theory of knowledge but one of understanding and wisdom. It asks questions like: given the facts of science, does God exist? If He does exist, what is His nature and purpose in creating us? Theology is the attempt of the frail human intellect to comprehend the mind of God through the revelations that He has given to us in the Holy Bible and interpreting what we see in nature. And it is hard work—as hard as understanding minds.

Dan Barker thinks that theology is the study of nothing. But we beg to differ. It is science that is the study of nothing, since the atheists believe that the cosmos popped out of absolutely nothing. He can talk to Lawrence Krauss to know what we are talking about.

Statement: Christians are atheists when it comes to believing other gods, why not go one step further?

Isn't this the story of the atheists and scientific materialists? First, they said the universe is made of four elements (earth, fire, air, and water) and then change their mind to say a hundred or so elements (of the Periodic Table,) then they said those elements are made up of quarks and leptons and now they say that all these subatomic particles popped out of nothing. According to them, we are a product of nothing.

How scientific and rational is that? The fact is that we are the product of the first cause and whatever science wants to label that first cause, we revere that entity as our Creator God. And this Creator had the power, order, and wisdom to create this vast cosmos and us. God is therefore, the root cause of our existence. The atheists can delude themselves that everything popped out of nothing, but they have no right to call it either rational or scientific.

Statement: Science is enough, we don't need God!

Enough for what? To create the universe? Are their equations some abracadabra spell that would bring the universe into being? Science is puerile commentary. It is a discovering of how the universe works and not inventing it. Who or what created the universe is the central question. Unfortunately, science cannot answer this question because of its causal methodology which relapses into a *reductio ad absurdum*. Its turtles all the way down for them.

Besides, what is so great about science? Give a toddler a bunch of preconfigured Lego blocks, some open space and time in her crèche, she will more or less figure out all the configurations that are possible. But the central question every atheist has to answer is where are they going to get the space, time, and the Lego blocks from? Out of nothing?

Finally, those who say that they don't need God are the ones who usually have come to God only for their needs and not for truth. If their needs are fulfilled elsewhere they won't care for the truth any longer. By making such grandiose statements, they have clearly demonstrated that they have no regard for values.

Statement: All religions are one, they take different paths to reach a common goal.

Such syncretism is hypocritical. This is more a political statement than a statement of truth. Those who believe that all religions are one, are making themselves wise and making God confused and incoherent. While the reality is exactly the opposite.

Why would He warn one about idolatry while let the other prostrate before idols? Why would He let one eat meat while tell the other to abstain? Why would He tell one not to worship the cow and allow others to worship it to the extent that they will kill others for it? Our God is not an author of confusion, it is man and his pride that is not allowing him to accept the one true God and religion.

It is the duty and purpose of humanity to seek the truth and choose the right religion instead of wasting time in pubs, malls, and in front of idiot boxes.

We have to treat all religions as scientific theories, examine which is closest to reality and accept it whole-heartedly. Christianity shines forth brilliantly in its conception of God. Ignore it at your peril.

Question: What about the Holocaust?

This tragedy is so great that we have to tread very carefully here. It is baffling to see many blame God for this while it was Hitler and the people who voted him to power that are solely responsible for this. But one may ask as to why God did not intervene? But would Hitler and his party oblige to good sense? Would Hitler have listened to his pastor? We don't think so. On one hand, we want the separation of church and state and on the other we want God to intervene when we are in trouble!

This great crime against humanity was committed by humanity itself. One which voted God out of the public square.

It is baffling to see many question God on this after deciding not to involve Him in their decision making. We should instead counter question the atheists. Where were the so called "rationalists" and "humanists" when this tragedy happened? Where were these cowards hiding? Where was the conscience of those scientists who armed the German war machine to conquer, bomb, destroy, and commit the biggest crime against innocent civilians? Let this be a grim reminder for mankind not to ignore God and His emissaries on earth. If we do not learn from history, we are doomed to repeat it.

Question: *What about those who are spiritual but not religious?*

This "spiritual but not religious" (SBNR) movement is as puerile as humanism without God. Having a form of Godliness but denying the power thereof. Without a code of conduct (religion,) moral ambiguity seeps into the society. Religion is the conscience keeper of nations and societies. In the case of SNBR, who decides their code of conduct? And on what authority? What if they differ among themselves? How are such differences resolved without a framework like religion which acts like a constitution? These are hard questions they need to answer.

Question: *What about the terrible acts of men and women mentioned in the Holy Bible?*

The Holy Bible is telling historical truth as it is, even when it is embarrassing. Many people have done terrible and abominable things in history and the Bible does not gloss over it. If the Israelites have sinned then it says bluntly that they have sinned and if they have reformed, it says that they have changed their ways. We should be careful not to confuse the descriptive elements with the prescriptive ones. Just because the Bible mentions that King David committed adultery does not mean that the Bible permits adultery. Many Muslims reject the Holy Bible because it does not censor the sinful nature of man. We would like to remind them that the Holy Bible is not a glossy mythical story, or a secret revelation in a cave but a historical book that does not gloss over the bad parts.

RECOMMENDED READING

Here are top seven books every Christian should read after The Holy Bible.

1. I don't have enough faith to be an Atheist – Norman L Geisler & Dr. Frank Turek
2. Signature in the Cell – Stephen C Meyer
3. Excavating the Bible – Yitzhak Meitlis
4. Jesus and the eye witnesses – Richard Bauckham
5. The End of Discovery – Russell Stannard
6. Jesus Among Other Gods – Ravi Zacharias
7. Christian Apologetics – Norman L Geisler

Recommended websites for every Christian Apologist.

1. www.reasonablefaith.org
2. www.crossexamined.org
3. https://apologetics315.com
4. www.reasons.org
5. www.biblicalarchaeology.org
6. www.illustramedia.com
7. www.Godandscience.org

50 books that every Christian Apologist should read.

1. Religion and Science – Ian G Barbour
2. Why there almost certainly is a God – Keith Ward

3. Darwin's Black Box – Michael J Behe
4. Is Religion Dangerous? – Keith Ward
5. The Facts of Life – Richard Milton
6. The Edge of Evolution – Michael J Behe
7. The Big Questions: Physics – Michael Brooks
8. Is Religion Irrational? – Keith Ward
9. The Science of God – Gerald L Schroeder
10. The Real Face of Atheism – Ravi Zacharias
11. Why Science does not disprove God – Amir D Aczel
12. What we cannot know – Marcus Du Sautoy
13. The Cell's Design – Fazale Rana
14. Not by chance – Dr. Lee Spetner
15. There is no a God – Antony Flew
16. The unknown Universe – Stuart Clark
17. We have no idea – Jorge Cham & Daniel Whiteson
18. Fashion, Faith & Fantasy – Roger Penrose
19. Evolution: A view from the twenty first century – James A Shapiro
20. The way of the cell – Franklin M Harold
21. New Scientist – The Big Questions series
22. The new evidence that demands a verdict - Josh Mcdowell
23. The Bible in the British Museum – T C Mitchell
24. The Matter Myth – Paul Davies & John Gribbin
25. Cosmic Jackpot – Paul Davies
26. The fire in the equations – Kitty Ferguson
27. The Goldilocks Enigma – Paul Davies
28. The Science Delusion – Rupert Sheldrake
29. The Devil's Delusion – David Berlinski
30. Undeniable – Dr. Douglas Axe
31. Zombie Science – Jonathan Wells
32. Uncommon Descent – William A Dembsky
33. Icons of Evolution – Jonathan Wells
34. Darwin's doubt – Stephen C Meyer
35. What is so great about Christianity? – Dinesh Desouza

36. God and Stephen Hawking – whose God is it anyway – John Lennox

37. God's undertaker – has science buried God? – John Lennox

38. Gunning for God – why the new atheists are missing the target – John Lennox

39. Does God Exist? – William Lane Craig

40. Evolution: A theory in crisis – Michael Denton

41. Reasonable faith: Christian truth and Apologetics – William Lane Craig

42. Why the universe is the way it is – Hugh Ross

43. The 5th miracle – Paul Davies

44. Improbable Planet – Hugh Ross

45. Forensic Faith – J Warner Wallace

46. Seeking Allah, finding Jesus – Nabeel Qureshi

47. The Case for a Creator – Lee Strobel

48. Stealing from God – Dr. Frank Turek

49. The Vital Question – Nick Lane

50. Origins of Life – Fazale Rana & Hugh Ross

BIBLIOGRAPHY AND REFERENCE

Various books, journals, websites and YouTube videos have been referred to while writing this book. In addition to the books below, I have also referred to scientific news magazines and journals which I have acknowledged within the book wherever I thought it was necessary. If I have missed anyone, please do let us know we will add your name to the list in the future editions of this book.

All quotes from The Holy Bible are from the *King James Version*

Aczel, Amir D., *Why Science Does Not Disprove God* (William Morrow 2015)

Al-Chalabi, Ammar and Turner, Martin R and Delamont, R Shane, *The Brain: A Beginner's Guide* (Oneworld Publications 2012)

Atkins, Peter, *Creation Revisited* (Penguin Books Ltd 1994)

Atkins, Peter, *On Being: A scientist's exploration of the great questions of existence* (Oxford University Press 2011)

Baggini, Julian, *Without God, is Everything Permitted?* (Quercus Editions Ltd 2014)

Baggott, Jim, *Farewell to Reality* (Constable & Robinson Ltd 2013)

Bauckham, Richard, *Jesus and the Eyewitnesses: The Gospels as Eyewitness Testimony* (Wm. B. Eerdmans Publishing Co. 2017)

Behe, Michael J., *Darwin's Black Box* (Free Press 2006)

Behe, Dr. Michael J., *The Edge of Evolution* (Free Press 2008)

Berlinski, David, *The Devil's Delusion* (Basic Books 2009)

Bronowski, Jacob, *Science and Human Values* (Faber & Faber 2011)

Brooks, Michael, *The Secret Anarchy of Science* (Profile Books Ltd. 2012)

Collins, Francis, *The Language of God* (Simon & Schuster UK 2007)

Coyne, Jerry A., *Faith versus Fact* (Penguin Books 2016)

Davies, Paul, *Cosmic Jackpot* (Orion Productions 2007)

Dawkins, Richard, *Climbing Mount Improbable* (Penguin UK 2006)

Dawkins, Richard, *The Blind Watchmaker* (Penguin UK 2006)

Dawkins, Richard, *The God Delusion* (Bantam Press 2006)

Dawkins, Richard, *The Selfish Gene* (Oxford University Press 1996)

Dawkins, Richard, *Science in the Soul* (Transworld Publishers 2017)

Dever, William G., *What Did the Biblical Writers Know & When Did They Know it?* (Wm. B. Eerdmans Publishing Co. 2002)

D'Souza, Dinesh, *What's so Great About Christianity* (Regnery Publishing Inc. 2008)

Du Sautoy, Marcus, *What we Cannot Know* (Fourth Estate 2016)

Ferguson, Kitty, *The Fire in the Equations: Science, Religion and the Search for God* (Bantam Press 1994)

Flew, Anthony, *There is a God: How the World's Most Notorious Atheist Changed His Mind* (HarperCollins 2008)

France, R. T., *The Evidence for Jesus* (Hodder and Stoughton 1999)

Fuller, Steve, *Dissent Over Descent* (Icon Books Ltd 2008)

Geisler, Norman L., *Christian Apologetics* (Baker Books 2004)

Gonzalez, Guillermo and Richards, Jay Wesley, *The Privileged Planet* (Regnery Publishing Inc 2004)

Grayling, A. C., *The God Argument* (Bloomsbury Publishing Plc 2014)

Grayling, A. C., *What is Good?* (Phoenix 2004)

Hitchens, Christopher, *God is Not Great* (Atlantic Books 2007)

Harari, Yuval Noah, *Sapiens: A brief History of Humankind* (Vintage Books 2017)

Harari, Yuval Noah, *Homo Deus: A Brief History of Tomorrow* (Vintage Books 2017)

Harold, Franklin M., *In Search of Cell History: The Evolution of Life's Building Blocks* (University of Chicago Press 2014)

Harris, Sam, *The Moral Landscape* (Free Press 2010)

Harris, Sam, *Letter to a Christian Nation* (Vintage Books 2008)

Kaiser Jr., Walter C., *The Old Testament Documents: Are They Reliable & Relevant?* (Inter Varsity Press 2003)

Kauffman, Stuart A., *The Origins of Order: Self-Organization and Selection in Evolution* (Oxford University Press 1993)

Krauss, Lawrence, *A Universe from Nothing: Why There Is Something Rather than Nothing* (Atria Books 2012)

Lane, Nick, *The Vital Question* (Profile Books Limited 2016)

Law, Stephen, Humanism: *A Very Short Introduction* (Oxford University Press 2011)

Malik, Kenan, *The Quest for a Moral Compass* (Atlantic Books Ltd 2014)

McDowell, Josh, *The New Evidence That Demands a Verdict* (Thomas Nelson Publishers 2011)

McGrath, Alister and McGarth, Joanna Collicutt, *The Dawkins Delusion* (Society for Promoting Christian Knowledge 2007)

Meitlis, Yitzhak, *Excavating the Bible: New Archaeological Evidence for the Historical Reliability of Scripture* (Eshel Books 2012)

Meyer, Stephen C., *Darwin's Doubt: The Explosive Origin of Animal Life and the Case for Intelligent Design* (HarperOne 2014)

Meyer, Stephen C., *Signature in the Cell* (HarperCollins 2009)

Milton, Richard, *The Facts of Life: Shattering the Myths of Darwinism* (Corgi Edition 1993)

Painter, Borden W. Jr., *The New Atheist Denial of History* (Palgrave Macmillan 2014)

Parker, Andrew, *The Genesis Enigma: Why the Bible is Scientifically Accurate* (Black Swan 2010)

Parrington, John., *The Deeper Genome: Why there is more to the human genome than meets the eye* (Oxford University Press 2015)

Penrose, Roger., *Fashion, Faith, and Fantasy in the New Physics of the Universe* (Princeton University Press 2016)

Pitre, Brant, *The Case for Jesus: The Biblical and Historical Evidence for Christ* (Crown Publishing Group 2016)

Potter, Christopher, *How to Make a Human Being* (Fourth Estate 2014)

Rana, Fazale, *Creating Life in the Lab* (Baker Books 2011)

Rana, Fazale, *The Cell's Design: How Chemistry Reveals the Creator's Artistry* (Baker Books 2008)

Rees, Martin, *Just Six Numbers* (Phoenix 2000)

Ridenour, Fritz, *So What's the Difference?* (Regal Books 2001)

Rose, Hilary and Rose, Steven, *Genes, Cells and Brains* (Foundation Books 2015)

Ross, Hugh, *Why the Universe is the Way it is* (Baker Books 2008)

Sanders, E. P., *The Historical Figure of Jesus* (Penguin Books 1995)

Sagan, Carl., *The Varieties of Scientific Experience: A Personal View of the Search for God* (Penguin Publishing Group 2006)

Schroeder, Gerald L., *Genesis and the Big Bang* (Bantam Books 1992)

Schroeder, Gerald L., *The Science of God* (Free Press 1997)

Shapiro, James A., *Evolution: A View from the 21st Century* (Pearson Education 2011)

Shermer, Michael, *The Moral Arc: How Science Makes Us Better People* (Henry Holt and Co. 2015)

Smolin, Lee, *The Trouble With Physics* (Penguin Books 2006)

Spector, Tim, *Identically Different* (Phoenix 2013)

Spetner, Dr. Lee, *Not by Chance!* (The Judaica Press, Inc. 1997)

Spetner, Dr. Lee, *The Evolution Revolution: Why Thinking People are Rethinking the Theory of Evolution* (The Judaica Press, Inc. 2014)

Staniforth, Maxwell and Louth, Andrew, *Early Christian Writings* (Penguin Classics 1987)

Stannard, Russell, *The End of Discovery* (Oxford University Press 2010)

Strobel, Lee, *The Case for Christ* (Zondervan Publishing 2006)

Turek, Frank and L. Geisler, Norman, *I Don't Have Enough Faith to be an Atheist* (Crossway 2004)

Ward, Keith, *Is Religion Dangerous?* (Lion Hudson plc 2006)

Ward, Keith, *Is Religion Irrational* (Lion Hudson plc 2011)

Ward, Keith, *Why There Almost Certainly is a God* (Lion Hudson plc 2008)

Warren, Rick, *The Purpose Driven Life* (Zondervan 2002)

Whiston, William, *The Works of Josephus* (Hendrickson Publishers 2006)

Wolpert, Lewis, *How We Live and Why We Die* (Faber & Faber Ltd 2009)

Yanai, Itai and Lercher, Martin, *The Society of Genes* (Harvard University Press 2016)

Zacharias, Ravi, *Jesus Among Other Gods: The Absolute Claims of the Christian Message* (Thomas Nelson Publishers 2001)

Zacharias, Ravi, *The End of Reason* (Zondervan 2008)

Zacharias, Ravi, *The Real Face of Atheism* (Baker Books 2004)

I would also like to mention countless articles in New Scientist and Biblical Archaeological Review magazines which I have referred to while I was researching for this book.

ACKNOWLEDGEMENTS

"But God hath chosen the foolish things of the world to confound the wise;..." I Corinthians 1:27

I would first of all like to thank my God for enabling me to share His revelations with others. I still vividly remember how one Centre Pastor prayed for me earnestly (more than twenty years ago in a youth camp) when I expressed my desire to write a book showing the flaws of evolution. I would therefore like to thank all the saints and believers who have prayed for me since. Without divine sanction and the prayers of His saints, this book would not have seen the light of the day. Their messages and admonitions have been like anointing oil on my head.

It is ironic and perhaps sad that the intended audience of this book is not the Eastern world (where Christianity is a minority) but the West which was once the stronghold of Christianity. Christianity in India owes much to the forefathers of those living in the West today, blessed perhaps because of the sacrifices that their forefathers had made. I would like to acknowledge their exemplary missionary work which has enlightened us of the truth in Christianity.

I was doing the final edits of this book in March, which is the month of my mother's birthday. Perhaps a reminder that I was fortunate to inherit the faith of my mother and the courage of my father. This unique combination I owe my parents. I would also like to thank my wife for her patience and forbearance while I was researching and writing this book (even though she does not approve of the general approach that I have taken to debunk atheism.) At the same time, I also have to apologize to her, my in-laws, and my own brother for not being an ideal husband and brother during the time I was writing this book.

I still remember how captivated my brother was by Carl Sagan's "Cosmos" and how it misled his young mind. I think our common interest in the existence of God was aroused when we saw a tome *Does God Exist?* written by Hans Küng in the personal library of our uncle (Late Rt. Rev. B. G. Prasada Rao) who was the former bishop of the (Anglican) Church of South India, Medak Diocese. Thankfully my brother was awakened from his dogmatic slumber of scientism and drugs after he attended the local theological college. I therefore have to thank all the Christian apologists out there, all my brothers-in-arms that are crusading against the deluded militant atheists. We deeply admire Christian apologists like Norman Geisler, Frank Turek, William Lane Craig, and Ravi Zacharias, whose writings we wholeheartedly recommend more than this book.

I would also like to apologize to everyone who may have been offended by what I said in this book. Especially when I make comparisons of Christianity with other religions. I would urge people of all religions to keep aside our differences and earnestly crusade against atheism before it becomes a bane to our society. At the same time, like my forefathers we should have a zeal for truth and be open minded enough to change our perception of God.

Although there may be copyrights attached to this book, one is encouraged to freely use the content without distorting its core message. Freely I have received and freely I give away. One is free to use the content of this revelation with one strong caveat: I reserve the right to withdraw its use if it is used for pure commercial gain, distorting, and misrepresenting Christianity or promoting any other religion.

I will end with a disclaimer. This book is solely my view and my view alone. My family is in no way responsible for its contents (my wife has not even read the draft of this book.) Neither does the church that I attend have anything to do with it since they would not approve of the combative approach of this book.

> "...ye should earnestly contend for the faith which was once delivered unto the saints." Jude 1:3.

Oscar Priyanand
March 2018
Secunderabad, India.

INDEX

V

W

Z

Printed in the United States
By Bookmasters